Sir Edmund Hillary

SAMUEL WILLARD CROMPTON

GREAT EXPLORERS

Jacques Cartier

James Cook

Hernán Cortés

Sir Francis Drake

Vasco da Gama

Sir Edmund Hillary

Robert de La Salle

Lewis and Clark

Ferdinand Magellan

Sir Ernest Shackleton

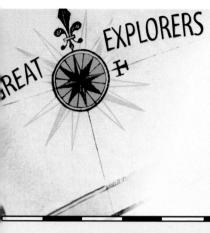

GREAT EXPLORERS

Sir Edmund Hillary

SAMUEL WILLARD CROMPTON

CHELSEA HOUSE
PUBLISHERS
An imprint of Infobase Publishing

GREAT EXPLORERS: SIR EDMUND HILLARY

Chelsea House
An imprint of Infobase Publishing
132 West 31st Street
New York, NY 10001

Library of Congress Cataloging-in-Publication Data
Crompton, Samuel Willard.
 Sir Edmund Hillary / Samuel Willard Crompton.
   p. cm. — (Great explorers)
 Includes bibliographical references and index.
 ISBN 978-1-60413-420-9 (hardcover)
 1. Hillary, Edmund, 1919-2008--Juvenile literature. 2. Mountaineers—New Zealand—Biography—Juvenile literature. 3. Mountaineering expeditions—Everest, Mount (China and Nepal)—History—Juvenile literature. 4. Everest, Mount (China and Nepal—Description and travel—Juvenile literature. I. Title. II. Series.
 GV199.92.H54C76 2009
 796.522092—dc22
 [B]   2009008688

CONTENTS

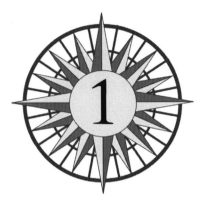

The High Ledge

IT WAS COLD ON THE LEDGE, ABOUT 20 DEGREES BELOW ZERO. The tent seemed frozen stiff, but at least it did not flap in the wind. The two men in the tent began to rouse themselves around three in the morning.

The Kiwi and the Sherpa

Dawn comes early in the High Himalaya, and it comes especially early on the slopes of Mount Everest, the world's highest place. While people in lower Tibet and lower Nepal see nothing but darkness, those on the slopes of the great mountains can see the first twinkling of dawn. So it was on May 29, 1953.

When thirty-three-year-old Edmund Hillary had awoken, he realized that the night oxygen had given out, making it harder to breathe in the little tent. Born in Auckland and raised in Tuakau, New Zealand, Hillary and his countrymen were known as "Kiwis," an affectionate term after the national bird of New Zealand.

On May 29, 1953, under the leadership of Brit John Hunt, New Zealand beekeeper Edmund Hillary and Sherpa Tenzing Norgay were immortalized when they became the first men to step foot on the summit of Mount Everest. Hillary and Tenzing became the most celebrated citizens of their respective countries, and they dedicated much of their lives to bettering the conditions of the Sherpas.

Thirty-nine-year-old Tenzing Norgay also found it difficult to breathe, but he was used to it, having grown up in the foothills near Mount Everest. In high altitude, people can get sick or even die due to the drop in air pressure, which makes it harder for oxygen to enter the circulatory system.

Tenzing was accustomed to people thinking he was Nepalese or Tibetan or Indian. Actually his ethnic identity was that of a Sherpa, the people that live in northeastern Nepal, close to Everest, the great mountain they call *Chomolungma* (meaning "Mountain So High No Bird Flies Over It"). For unknown reasons, Sherpas are able to withstand high altitude better than others.

Hillary and Tenzing had not known each other very long, less than three months, but they had become a formidable climbing team. The six-foot-three-inch Hillary usually led the way, with the five-foot-eight-inch Tenzing providing the *belay* ("anchor") to the climbing team. Less than a month earlier, Tenzing had saved Hillary's life when the New Zealand adventurer hurtled down a crevasse on a block of ice. Tenzing tightened the rope that bound them, allowing Hillary to climb out of the sheer-walled ice chasm. It was as important as life and death that the 11-man British team that was attempting to "conquer" Mount Everest (most of the team members quietly acknowledged that one could not truly conquer such a mountain, that the best they could do was to persuade it to relent) looked out for one another.

Surveying the World

Hillary pulled the frozen tent flaps back, and both men slowly emerged onto the tiny ledge where they had spent the night. They had slept at about 27,900 feet, the highest that human beings had ever done, but their great mission was not yet complete. Mount Everest is variously estimated at 29,002 to 29,035 feet, so they had about 1,100 feet still to go, and those could be among the most treacherous of all.

Tenzing came up behind Hillary, pointed to the southwest, and said, "Thyangboche."

Hillary knew, at once, what he meant. The famed Buddhist monastery of Thyangboche lay south of Everest, while its equally famed brother monastery, Rongbuck, was to the north. Hillary's gaze followed Tenzing's finger. Three years later, Hillary described what he saw in his autobiography *High Adventure*:

> "Sure enough, there in the great wide Imja valley we could see the faint outlines of the monastery perched in its lovely setting on top of a great spur. It was about 17,000 feet

below us. Already we knew that the monks down there would be performing their early morning devotions and perhaps, as they had promised to do, they were at this moment turning their eyes up toward us and praying for our well-being."

Hillary and Tenzing looked again at the vast world that was beginning to be revealed by early daylight. They knew, as

The location of the Thyangboche monastery in the Solo Khumbu region and its two important religious festivals make it a popular stop for inhabitants and climbers headed to Mount Everest's base camp. Its direct view of Mount Everest makes it one of the most beautiful places in the world. On January 19, 1989, the Thyangboche Monastery and School was destroyed by fire. The Hillary Trust raised money to rebuild it, and a formal opening was held in September 1993.

few men had before, how sublime the Himalayan views could be. They knew that they stood on the shoulders of giants who had come before them, men like George Mallory and Andrew Irvine and Eric Shipton and Charles G. Bruce. They knew that this was their moment, the day on which the British expedition of 1953 would succeed or fail. They turned back to the tent.

Ready, Set, Stop

As soon as they reentered the tent, Hillary and Tenzing found something amiss. Hillary, who had taken his boots off before going to sleep the night before, found that they were frozen solid. Tenzing had, wisely, kept his boots on during the extremely cold night.

Hillary spent the next hour warming his boots over the Primus stove, which the team had lugged all the way up to 27,900 feet. There had been times when the team had cursed the weight of the stove, but at this point they saw it was a complete necessity. Tenzing knew best of all what an asset this stove was, for one year earlier, while climbing with a Swiss expedition, he had reached a similar altitude and they had had no stove on that last day.

After an hour, Hillary's boots had warmed up. Hillary had to endure the acrid smell of burnt leather, and the boots were badly singed on the edges, but it seemed to have been worth it, for at least now he could climb.

Setting Out

Hillary and Tenzing dressed very warmly for what they knew would be a difficult ascent. At least there was no wind.

They put on heavy wool clothing, black overcoats, and three pairs of gloves each: one silk, one wool, and one wetproof. They had almost none of the special type of equipment mountain climbers would use a generation or two later. Around his ice axe, Tenzing had tightly woven four national flags: those of the Kingdom of Nepal, the Republic of India, Great Britain, and the United Nations.

"All ready?" Hillary asked.

"Ah cha. Ready," Tenzing replied.

This was the moment. Seven British expeditions had come and gone over the past 30 years. Hundreds of men had attempted to climb the world's highest mountain. But it had all come down to the Kiwi and the Sherpa. It was now or never, do or die.

Bees and Skis

ALTHOUGH "DOWN UNDER" REFERS TO AUSTRALIA AND ITS
people, it would be a more appropriate reference for New
Zealand and the Kiwis. New Zealand truly is the "bottom" of
the Eastern Hemisphere. One has to travel all the way to South
America (Auckland, New Zealand, is about on the same lati-
tude as Rio de Janeiro, Brazil) to find land and peoples as truly
"south" as the Kiwis of New Zealand.

The Hillarys and Clarks

Edmund (Ed) Hillary was born in Auckland on July 20, 1919,
to Percival Augustus Hillary and Gertrude Clark. When Ed was
born, Percival and Gertrude already had one child, a daughter
named June. Another son, Rex, followed a year after Ed's birth.

About the time that Percival Hillary met Gertrude Clark, in
1910, the total population in New Zealand reached one million.
Gertrude came from a family of merchants and schoolteachers

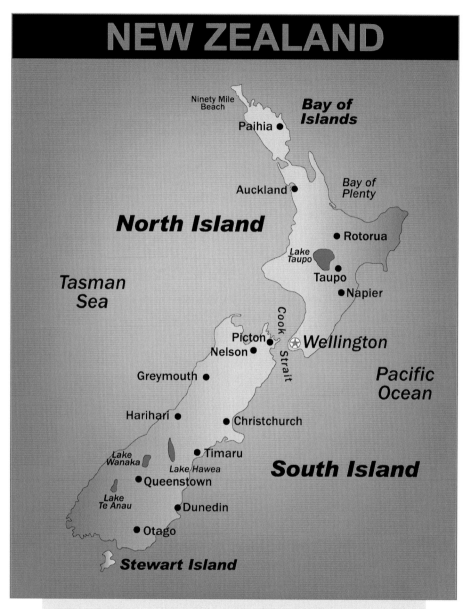

NEW ZEALAND

Ninety Mile Beach

Bay of Islands

Paihia ●

Auckland ●

Bay of Plenty

North Island

● Rotorua

Lake Taupo

Taupo ●

●Napier

Tasman Sea

Cook Strait

Picton ●

Nelson ●

⊛ *Wellington*

Greymouth ●

Pacific Ocean

Harihari ●

● Christchurch

● Timaru

Lake Wanaka

Lake Hawea

South Island

● Queenstown

Lake Te Anau

● Dunedin

● Otago

⤳ *Stewart Island*

Edmund Hillary was raised in rural Tuakau, south of Auckland. The total land area of New Zealand is 103,738 square miles (268,680 sq km), a little smaller than that of Italy or Japan and a little larger than the United Kingdom. New Zealand is one of the most recently settled major landmasses, with the first settlers arriving sometime between 700 and 2,000 years ago.

who had prospered from the lumber boom on New Zealand's northwest coast in the late nineteenth century. She grew up in more genteel circumstances than Percival, and, throughout their long lives together, she would act as the "civilizing" influence on him. Percival and Gertrude were optimistic about the future. They would have married sooner if the Great War had not intervened to throw off their plans.

World War I

Today we call it the First World War, but in 1914–1918 people called it simply "the Great War." England and her many colonies (including New Zealand) were part of the Allied Powers, while Germany, Austria, Bulgaria, and the Ottoman Empire (present-day Turkey) formed the Central Powers.

When the Great War began, New Zealanders were eager to enlist to demonstrate their patriotism. They considered themselves British first and New Zealanders second. Percival joined the infantry, and in 1915 he was part of the Australian New Zealand Army Corps (ANZAC) group sent to attack Istanbul, the capital of the Ottoman Empire.

They never got there. The British, Australians, and New Zealanders landed at a peninsula called Gallipoli, starting a yearlong campaign that ended in disaster. Australians and New Zealanders still proudly celebrate ANZACs Day (April 25) as a red-letter event in their national histories, but for men like Percival, Gallipoli was a trial in the extreme.

Wounded in the nose on the fourth day of battle, Percival managed to rejoin his unit, but superior officers soon deemed him unfit to serve. In 1916, he was sent home to New Zealand. Two weeks later, Percival married Gertrude Clark.

The 1920s

The three Hillary children—June, Ed, and Rex—grew up very much in awe of their father. It was not that he was very large or very strong but that he had within him a tremendous will that carried him through all sorts of difficulties. Percival had been a journalist before the Great War, and he returned to that occupation in 1916. He also developed a sideline passion: beekeeping.

Honey is a popular condiment in New Zealand, and the national government sponsored a program for returning veterans to enter the business. Percival worked as a journalist for several years, but he eventually became a full-time beekeeper, and his sons learned the business from him.

Ed Hillary grew up in the small village of Tuakua, about 45 miles south of Auckland, where his father started the family's first hives and apiaries. Ed walked to school barefoot, but this was typical of New Zealand country children at the time. He was small for his age, and his elementary-school years were painful. Shy and awkward, he did not make many friends. Ed really had only two playmates, his brother and sister, but the Hillary family was a lively one. His mother played the piano, his father told excellent stories of adventure, and there was plenty of laughter.

As the 1920s ended, Ed Hillary was an unremarkable boy, living in a largely unnoticed part of the world. There was nothing wrong with this—many New Zealanders cherished their distance from the wider world—but the young boy dreamed of adventure. Sometimes he walked with a stick and threw stones, imagining himself as a grand adventurer: a knight with a sword or a soldier with a catapult, for example.

The Great Depression

The Great Depression began with the American stock market crash of October 1929, and it effects reached most of the Western, industrialized world. Because its economy had a balance between industry and agriculture, for a while New Zealand was able to avoid the hardships that other countries were facing. Nonetheless, by 1934, when Ed was 15, New Zealand could no longer evade the Depression. It was a time of enormous stress, hunger, and despair. About 100,000 men were out of work, and children had to leave school and take work in order to help the family survive.

New Zealanders were torn between their pioneering, adventurous heritage and their concern for the less fortunate. Many New Zealanders believed the Depression would have to naturally run its course, no matter what the cost. The Hillarys were not among them. Though they cherished stories of the willpower of their ancestors, the Hillarys were among those who believed only the state had the power and money to set the economy right. When the Labour Party won the general elections of 1935, New Zealand was set in a new direction: that of moderate socialism.

Health insurance and old-age pensions were guaranteed for all. The state paid large subsidies to industries to employ workers, and colleges and universities also received grants to attract more students. Between 1935–1940, New Zealand was transformed from a pioneer country with a rather macho attitude to a modern, industrial nation with a socialistic outlook. The Hillarys supported the changes.

Work and Play

Ed Hillary went to work for his father at an early age, and by the time he was 15, he had learned how to do a man's job with the bees. His father paid Ed and his brother very little, just enough to keep them working. It was about this time that Ed discovered one of the great loves of his life, recounted later in *High Adventure*:

> "I saw my first snow at midnight when we stepped off the train at the National Park station. There wasn't much of it, but it was a tremendous thrill and before long snowballs, hard as iron, were flying through the air....For ten glorious days we skied and played on the lower slopes of

the mountain [Ruapehu] and I don't think I ever looked toward the summit. We had been told the upper parts of the mountain were dangerous and I viewed them with

NEW ZEALAND'S MANY FACES

Most people living in the Northern Hemisphere know very little about New Zealand. To the extent that they think about the lands Down Under, they think of the hot desert and scrub brush of Australia. Located about 1,400 miles east of Australia, New Zealand could not be more different.

The country is divided into three islands: North Island, South Island, and Stewart Island. Ed Hillary grew up on North Island and did not see South Island until his late teens. This was not unusual, for the two "big" islands are very different places. North Island receives trade winds from Hawaii and the Solomon Islands, while South Island and Stewart Island get some of their weather from Antarctica.

North Island is best known for its fabulous beaches and its three volcanic mountains, each of which is over 8,000 feet. North Island also has a larger population than the other two. South Island, the biggest island in New Zealand, is best known for the Southern Alps, which run northeast to southwest, creating a spine of the island. They are capped by spectacular Mount Cook, which towers over the Tasman Glacier. South Island has only about one quarter of New Zealand's population, while approximately 76 percent of New Zealand's inhabitants live on North Island. With slightly fewer than 400 people living on Stewart Island, this small island truly can feel like the "bottom" of the world.

Locations in New Zealand, including the Southern Alps, have been featured in several films, including the *Lord of the Rings* trilogy (2001-2003), *The Chronicles of Narnia: The Lion, the Witch and the Wardrobe* (2005), and *Bridge to Terabithia* (2007). Today, New Zealand has become more recognizable for millions of people around the globe.

respect and fear....I returned home in a glow of fiery enthusiasm for the sun and the cold and the snow— especially the snow!"

Ed's natural athleticism now began to emerge. The awkward boy who had once been ridiculed in school began to take on the long, angular lines for which he would be known. Sometime in his early teens, Ed had a growth spurt that eventually took him all the way to six-foot-three. While his new height and strength did not diminish his feelings of shyness and inadequacy, Ed certainly was not one to be bullied. Not even by his father.

Ed's confidence grew as he proved himself, time and again, both on the ski slopes and with the beehives. By 1939, Ed was 20 years old and no longer a boy. That was also the year the world began another life-changing war.

Men and Mountains

NEW ZEALAND GREETED THE START OF WORLD WAR II WITH less enthusiasm than it had World War I. In 1914, New Zealanders felt they had something to prove about their worthiness as subjects of the British Empire. In 1939, they felt that the empire was, perhaps, relying a bit too much on them.

Enlistment and Conscription

Economic and defensive considerations motivated New Zealand, a former British colony, to get involved in the war. Many New Zealanders saw the United Kingdom as the "mother country"; their reliance on Great Britain meant that a threat to Great Britain was a threat to New Zealand. Still, at the beginning of the war when New Zealand's government wished to rely on enlistments, it found many of its young men reluctant to go off to war. Hitler and the Nazis seemed like a very far-off threat to those living Down Under. In 1940, Prime Minister Peter Fraser announced a draft.

Ed and Rex Hillary were not the gung-ho type, at least not when it came to military conflict. From family stories they knew that their father, Percival, had never been the same after he returned from the First World War. The disastrous Gallipoli campaign had darkened his outlook on life. The Hillary family were pacifists (opposed to violence) and were open to different religious groups in the 1930s. Even so, Ed was prepared to go overseas and do his part. Applying to the Royal New Zealand Air Force, he hoped to become a navigator.

Much to his surprise, Hillary learned that his father had received an exemption from military service for him based on the importance of the bee industry. Hillary returned to working at his father's company and occasionally to skiing, but he was dismayed to learn that Rex had been drafted. Only one military exemption was allowed per family.

Rex applied for status as a conscientious objector. A conscientious objector is someone who refuses to comply with a legal obligation based on moral, religious, or ethical grounds. New Zealand's government was unsympathetic to conscientious objectors, however, so Rex spent almost four years in a special detention facility. Meanwhile, the pressure was on Ed to keep the family bee business in operation.

When the two brothers, along with their father, ran the business together, the business went smoothly. With their father getting older, and with Rex in a detention camp, it was up to Ed to carry the brunt of the work. The family now owned more than 1,600 beehives, and Ed stepped up to the plate, practically jogging from one beehive to the next. This constant activity got him into good shape; few of the men he later climbed with had such a demanding job at lower altitudes.

Although Ed continued to have mixed feelings about military service, in 1944 he again applied to the Royal Air Force. This time he was accepted, and he soon entered navigation training.

Meeting the Yanks

Hillary was sent to the Solomon Islands, where he met his first "Yanks," as New Zealanders called Americans. By the autumn of 1944, it was almost certain that the Allied forces would defeat the Axis powers.

In the spring of 1945, just as World War II was coming to an end, Hillary and a fellow navigator were involved in a serious boating accident. There was an explosion and both men had to jump out. They suffered serious burns. Hillary and his mate spent three weeks in an American hospital on the island of Guadalcanal and then were released, much earlier than the doctors expected. Hillary returned home and was released from the military in the autumn of 1945.

A New Country

Historian Michael King has described the changes that came to New Zealand in the wake of the Second World War:

> "The war might have been over in 1945, but many of the conditions of war prevailed. In particular, New Zealand and the United Kingdom [England, Scotland, and Northern Ireland] remained short of some foodstuffs....Sugar, tea and meat were rationed here until 1948, butter and petrol until 1950. In spite of this, New Zealanders contributed generously to government sponsored appeals for food for Britain."

Ed Hillary's family was beginning to show signs of change. His sister, June, had become a successful schoolteacher and was thinking about going to England. His brother, Rex, released from detention camp, was engaged to be married.

The Hillarys were a small microcosm of a large change that was sweeping New Zealand. The country that had been content as an appendage of the motherland was beginning to show signs of real independence. In 1945, at the United

Nations, Prime Minister Fraser objected to the creation of a "Great Power veto," meaning that a vote by Great Britain, France, China, Russia, or the United States could effectively block the will of the General Assembly.

Hillary was largely apolitical in the years after World War II, so what he thought of these matters is unknown. He now focused on a new passion: mountains.

Mount Cook

Standing well over 12,000 feet, Mount Cook is the most immense part of the very impressive skyline of the Southern Alps on South Island in New Zealand. Mount Cook consists of three summits: the Low Peak, the Middle Peak, and the High Peak. The Tasman Glacier lies to its east, and the Hooker Glacier is to its west. The first recorded attempt to climb it was made in 1882, and the first successful climb was made in 1894 by New Zealanders Tom Fyfe, James Clarke, and George Graham. Not until 1947 had anyone made the difficult South Ridge ascent to the Low Peak.

In 1947, Hillary became friends with Harry Ayres, the best climber in New Zealand at the time. Ayres had perfected the skill of hacking through ice to create steps. In February 1947 they went up the South Ridge of Mount Cook, the first climbers ever to do so. This achievement boosted Hillary's confidence, and he branched out into other areas of endurance. In his second autobiography, *View from the Summit*, Hillary wrote:

> I started to do more and more climbing in the winter and became an experienced ski-mountaineer, traveling with a variety of companions. One winter Jack McBurney and I spent a month or so together. First we had two weeks shooting deer....Then we went gold panning up the Cook River in freezing conditions. We certainly didn't get much gold, so our enthusiasm for this faded rather quickly.

In 1939, Hillary made his first climb, to Mount Ollivier in New Zealand. In 1947 and 1949, he returned to the Southern Alps to climb Mount Cook, New Zealand's tallest mountain (*above*). Ascending the Southern Alps helped Hillary develop his climbing skills in preparation for Everest.

Coming back from the gold expedition, Hillary and his companion nearly froze to death. Luckily, one of them noticed the developing signs of hypothermia (abnormally low body temperature that becomes life threatening if below 32.2°C/90°F), and they were able to ward it off. During this time,

Hillary was turning an already wiry physique into one capable of extraordinary endurance. He skied, hunted, and prospected during the winter and worked with his brother, Rex, with the bees during the spring and summer. The two young men had now become vital to the business, and their father had to pay them more than in the past, but he still kept as tight a leash as possible on them.

FIRST TRIP "HOME"

New Zealanders had gained full political independence by the late 1940s, but cultural connections to the British motherland remained strong. Many New Zealanders still referred to England as "home."

In the spring of 1950, Ed was working hard with his brother, Rex, when he received a rather urgent telegram from his parents in London. They were in England to celebrate the wedding of Ed's sister, June, to an English doctor. Although Ed's mother wanted to tour Europe, his father was reluctant to do any traveling. They asked Ed to join them in Europe. Ed dropped his work at the apiary and boarded a passenger ship to London for his first visit to the motherland in the summer of 1950.

It was a glorious time to see England. The country had largely recovered from the Second World War and there was a sense of pride among the English. Hillary hit all of the usual tourist sites, but he was even more anxious to climb some of the European mountains. After a few weeks of driving his parents around southern and central Europe, he had his first look at the Swiss and Austrian Alps.

He found them no more difficult to climb than the Southern Alps of New Zealand. Perhaps he said so too loudly and too often, for he found it difficult to develop friendships with the Swiss mountain guides. Still, he came away from the summer trip with the resolution to do more climbing in other parts of the world.

Rex married in the late 1940s, and he and his wife welcomed Ed into their home. Living with his brother, plus the wages he earned at the apiary, allowed Hillary to pursue his passions more than before. During a conversation with his friend George Lowe in 1950, Hillary's future path was determined. As they came down the Tasman Glacier in the Southern Alps, Lowe asked Hillary, "Have you ever thought of going to the Himalayas, Ed?"

He had indeed.

Mukut Parbat

Hillary joined a large New Zealand expedition, with as many as 20 climbers. Funds proved scarce—and experienced climbers even scarcer—so the group was reduced to four men: Hillary, his friend George Lowe, Earle Riddiford, and Ed Cotter. Tensions led to disagreements on a number of occasions. The problem was that Riddiford considered himself the leader of the group, while Hillary and Lowe thought all four men were on equal terms. Nevertheless, the group managed to leave New Zealand in the spring of 1951. They took the "flying boat," as the plane was called because it was designed to take off and land on water, from Auckland to Sydney, Australia, then connected to an ocean liner going to India. Before too long, they were in the Garhwal Himalaya, in northwestern India.

Although all four men were good climbers, none had experience in the Himalaya. As they approached Mukut Parbat (23,760 feet/7,242 meters)—which is part of Kamet, the third-highest mountain range in India—they experienced some trepidation. They did not possess the kind of winter equipment that is routine for major mountain climbing today, and they did not have a guide who knew the mountain. What they did learn very quickly was that it was essential to hire locals to carry their equipment to the lower reaches of the mountain.

In the 1950s, mountaineering equipment was bulky, heavy, and prone to malfunction. When the British Everest team began its quest, Hillary's pack weighed about 59 pounds. By the time he and Tenzing reached their last camp, they were carrying about 39 pounds. Pictured is the equipment used by Hillary when he summited Everest on May 29, 1953; it is housed in a Christchurch, New Zealand, museum.

Hillary and his mates soon fell in love with the Himalaya. What they could see in front of them was the endless challenge of mountain after mountain. What they could not see (lacking the satellite photography of today) was that the Himalaya form a crown over the top of India, Pakistan, Nepal, and Burma (present-day Myanmar), extending about 1,500 miles (2,414 kilometers) from east to west. The majestic Himalaya actually change the climate, preventing the rich, moisture-laden monsoon from reaching the high plateau of Tibet. One of the most astonishing features of the Himalaya is the difference between the southern slopes, many of which are moist and rich in vegetation, and the northern ones, which are usually barren.

The New Zealand team—the first of its type in the Himalaya—experienced many difficulties. At more than 23,700 feet, Mukut Parbat is not one of the greatest peaks, but it requires a fighting spirit and a team willing to work together. Unfortunately, the group was lacking in teamwork. Hillary and Lowe were nearly always in the lead, but at a critical point on the last day of climbing, they paused and Riddiford and a Sherpa passed them. Later that afternoon, Riddiford reached the summit of Mukut Parbat, a triumph denied Hillary and Lowe by the weather.

Hillary and Lowe were bitterly disappointed, but there was consolation when they arrived at their lodgings. A short cablegram had arrived. It read: "Permission for any two of you to join mission to enter Nepal, bringing own food and supplies." The cablegram was from Eric Shipton, one of the most famous names in mountaineering.

The four New Zealanders looked at one another and spent the better part of a day arguing over who should take part in this opportunity. Riddiford had succeeded on Mukut Parbat, which he thought should guarantee his selection. Hillary and Lowe had consistently proved themselves to be the best climbing team: They believed that spoke for itself. Cotter was less vocal but no less desirous of being chosen.

Finally they came to a compromise: Hillary and Riddiford would go. Years later, Hillary remembered the accusatory look on Lowe's face as he drove off. At that moment neither of them could know that they would climb together in the future on the grandest stage of all.

A Quick Journey

Eric Shipton's cable had suggested speed, so Hillary and Riddiford moved quickly. What they understood was that Shipton intended to approach Mount Everest from its southern side, something never done before. They had to get there quickly.

Hillary and Riddiford traveled on two rail journeys that carried them across northern India. Even so, they arrived at the rendezvous too late. Shipton had left four days earlier. Undaunted, Hillary and Riddiford made a set of daring river crossings to catch up. As they came close to the campsite, Hillary had feelings of insecurity. These were Englishmen, after all, not informal New Zealanders. For all that he knew, they might shave every day and dress formally for dinner. If so, he and Riddiford would be sorely out of their element. Then came the thrilling moment as they spotted Eric Shipton puffing on his pipe. Hillary described his relief in *High Adventure*: "As we came into the room four figures rose to meet us. My first feeling was one of relief. I have rarely seen a more disreputable bunch and my visions of changing for dinner faded away forever."

They had come to the right place.

The Southern Approach

EUROPEANS CALL IT MOUNT EVEREST IN HONOR OF THE LEADER of the British survey in India, but the Nepali Sherpas call it *Chomolungma*, which means "Mountain So High No Bird Flies Over It." In either case, it is easy to recognize Mount Everest as the greatest mountain in the world.

Lay of the Land

Everest lies in the northeastern section of the 1,500-mile-long (2,414 kilometers) Himalaya mountain chain, which stretches from Pakistan to Myanmar. Local people, especially the Sherpas, have known of Mount Everest for centuries, but Europeans only became aware of it in the 1850s after the British survey team identified it as Mountain XV. In 1865, it was renamed after Sir George Everest, the leader of the team.

Mount Everest, the highest mountain on Earth, towers over its neighbors, but it has four close competitors. Mount Lhotse

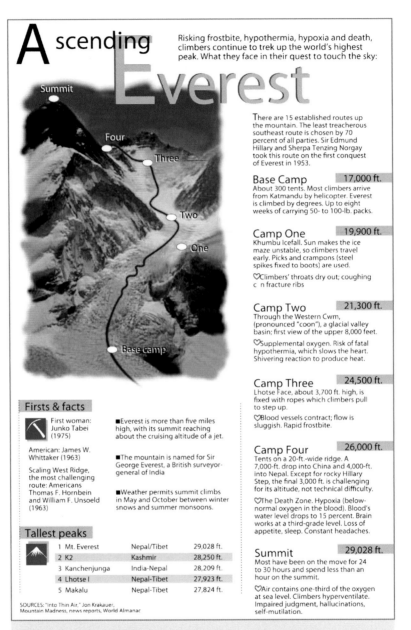

Ascending Everest

Risking frostbite, hypothermia, hypoxia and death, climbers continue to trek up the world's highest peak. What they face in their quest to touch the sky:

Summit

Four

Three

Two

One

Base camp

There are 15 established routes up the mountain. The least treacherous southeast route is chosen by 70 percent of all parties. Sir Edmund Hillary and Sherpa Tenzing Norgay took this route on the first conquest of Everest in 1953.

Base Camp   17,000 ft.
About 300 tents. Most climbers arrive from Katmandu by helicopter. Everest is climbed by degrees. Up to eight weeks of carrying 50- to 100-lb. packs.

Camp One   19,900 ft.
Khumbu Icefall. Sun makes the ice maze unstable, so climbers travel early. Picks and crampons (steel spikes fixed to boots) are used.

♡Climbers' throats dry out; coughing c n fracture ribs

Camp Two   21,300 ft.
Through the Western Cwm, (pronounced "coon"), a glacial valley basin; first view of the upper 8,000 feet.

♡Supplemental oxygen. Risk of fatal hypothermia, which slows the heart. Shivering reaction to produce heat.

Camp Three   24,500 ft.
Lhotse Face, about 3,700 ft. high, is fixed with ropes which climbers pull to step up.

♡Blood vessels contract; flow is sluggish. Rapid frostbite.

Camp Four   26,000 ft.
Tents on a 20-ft.-wide ridge. A 7,000-ft. drop into China and 4,000-ft. into Nepal. Except for rocky Hillary Step, the final 3,000 ft. is challenging for its altitude, not technical difficulty.

♡The Death Zone. Hypoxia (below-normal oxygen in the blood). Blood's water level drops to 15 percent. Brain works at a third-grade level. Loss of appetite, sleep. Constant headaches.

Summit   29,028 ft.
Most have been on the move for 24 to 30 hours and spend less than an hour on the summit.

♡Air contains one-third of the oxygen at sea level. Climbers hyperventilate. Impaired judgment, hallucinations, self-mutilation.

Firsts & facts

First woman: Junko Tabei (1975)

American: James W. Whittaker (1963)

Scaling West Ridge, the most challenging route: Americans Thomas F. Hornbein and William F. Unsoeld (1963)

■Everest is more than five miles high, with its summit reaching about the cruising altitude of a jet.

■The mountain is named for Sir George Everest, a British surveyor-general of India

■Weather permits summit climbs in May and October between winter snows and summer monsoons.

Tallest peaks

1	Mt. Everest	Nepal/Tibet	29,028 ft.
2	K2	Kashmir	28,250 ft.
3	Kanchenjunga	India-Nepal	28,209 ft.
4	Lhotse I	Nepal-Tibet	27,923 ft.
5	Makalu	Nepal-Tibet	27,824 ft.

SOURCES: "Into Thin Air," Jon Krakauer, Mountain Madness, news reports, World Almanac

There are 15 established routes up the mountain, with the southeast route being the most commonly used. Climbers begin their trip at Base Camp (17,000 feet). They will then make their dangerous climb to four camps (Hillary's team had nine), each more dangerous than the last. Ironically, descending Mount Everest can be even more treacherous than the climb to the summit.

(fourth-highest mountain in the world at 27,940 feet/8,516 meters) and Mount Nuptse (twentieth-highest mountain at 25,770 feet/7,855 meters) are within two miles of Everest. Makalu (fifth-highest mountain at 27,762 feet/8,462 meters) and Cho Oyu (sixth-highest mountain at 26,906 feet/8,201 meters) are within 10 and 20 miles, respectively. Part of Mount Everest's

"BECAUSE IT IS THERE"

That was George Mallory's reply to a *New York Times* reporter who asked why he wanted to climb Mount Everest. The reporter suspected that this was a phrase that would become historic. Born in Mobberley, England, in 1880, Mallory had refined his climbing in the Swiss Alps and in Wales. His love of adventure drew him to the Himalaya. As part of the 1923 British expedition, he had high hopes of reaching the summit in 1924.

Compared to the mountain-climbing equipment used today, the equipment available to the British team of 1924 was laughable. Mallory, Irvine, and the others had no special clothing or shoes. In fact, they looked almost as if they were out for a jaunt in the mountains of their beloved Wales. Their clothing consisted of a base layer, inner layer, and outer layer, and their equipment included a cotton tent, an eiderdown-filled sleeping bag, a wooden-handled ice axe, and three cylinders of oxygen (28 pounds in weight). They also wore a helmet, goggles, and boots with nails on the soles to prevent slipping. Today, the clothing is designed to withstand extreme cold and wind, and equipment is made of the highest-quality material. It is a wonder how they managed to do what they did with such equipment.

On June 8, 1924, Mallory and his climbing partner, Andrew Irvine, attempted to climb Mount Everest via the North Col route (like all expeditions before 1951). They never returned

(Continues)

(Continued)

to camp, and for 75 years they were missing somewhere high up on the mountain. Until 1999, when the BBC and the television show *Nova* sponsored the Mallory and Irvine Research Expedition, several expeditions had been unsuccessful in finding them. Within hours of the start of the 1999 expedition, Mallory's frozen, excellently preserved body was found at 26,760 feet. Irvine's remains were never located.

To this day, controversy surrounds the 1924 expedition. Did these two intrepid men reach the summit, only to die on the way down? Mallory's daughter has said that her father had carried a photograph of his wife with the intention of leaving it on the summit. When Mallory's body was recovered, the photo was not found. Could he have left it there and fallen on the way down? Second, Mallory's snow goggles were found in his pocket, usually an indication that Mallory and Irvine made a push for the summit and were descending after sunset. Given their known departure time and movements, if they had not attempted to reach the summit they would not have still been out at nightfall.

The speculation continues, but most advance the theory that the pair failed to reach the summit just short of their goal. Whichever the case, Mallory and Irvine set a standard for future Everest expeditions to follow, and their names endure for all time. Indeed, Mallory lent Welsh names to some of the geography around Mount Everest. He used *cwm* (pronounced coon) to describe the great holding place, or chamber, between Mount Everest and other mountains, and he used *col* (pronounced kawl) to describe the horizontal space between Mount Everest and the Lhotse Face. These are the names still used today.

inaccessibility is due to the surrounding great mountains and the glaciers that exist between them. To get to Mount Everest, one must first navigate lesser mountains and all sorts of serious dangers.

The British had taken the lead in Mount Everest exploration with their first expedition in 1921. It was followed by six others. Until 1951, all of the British teams approached Everest from its northern, or Tibetan, side. This made geographic sense as there were fewer peaks from that direction, and some of the British climbers (notably George Mallory and Sandy Irvine) came very close to reaching Mount Everest's summit. Changes in international policy, however, made it necessary to try Mount Everest from the southern side.

Eric Shipton was one of Hillary's heroes. Shipton, the only veteran of all four 1930s expeditions, found the route that Hillary and Tenzing would follow to the summit of Everest. Shipton's climbing style, which now embodies pure alpine climbing—using small teams and very little equipment and moving quickly—was rejected by the British expedition committee. He was dropped as leader of the 1953 Everest expedition, thereby killing his lifelong dream of reaching the top.

A series of aerial photographs of the area surrounding Mt. Everest taken in 1935 had been gathering dust in the archives of the Royal Geographic Society. In 1950, a young doctor named Michael Ward found them and presented them to the society. That same year, the Dalai Lama closed off access to Tibet after it was invaded by the People's Republic of China. Mountaineers were forced to look for alternative routes to Mount Everest. It made perfect sense to attempt a survey of the southern approaches to Everest, on the Nepal side of the mountain. This task was given to Eric Shipton.

Born in Ceylon (present-day Sri Lanka) in 1907, Shipton was already the veteran of four British expeditions to Everest and a hero to the young Ed Hillary. Granted permission in the summer of 1951, Shipton and four other Englishmen arrived in southern Nepal in September, where they were soon joined by Hillary and Riddiford.

Solo Khumbu

Shipton, Hillary, and the others made their way through southeast Nepal, the land the Sherpas call Solo Khumbu. If there is a place on Earth that resembles Shangri-La, it is somewhere in this section of Nepal, where rhododendrons blossom and ice peaks tower over all. The contrast between the lush vegetation on the ground and the starkness at the top had mesmerized Eric Shipton for many years. It now intrigued Hillary.

The Sherpa people had lived in the Solo Khumbu for about 450 years. Originally from Tibet, over time they had migrated to the southern side of the great Himalayan mountain chain. By the time Hillary arrived, in 1951, the Sherpas had begun to earn a living, however modest, by acting as porters for European expeditions to Everest and other mountains in the vicinity. In his first descriptions of the Solo Khumbu, Hillary paid more attention to the natural beauty than to the charms of its people. Eventually, this would change, as he became one of the Sherpas' strongest supporters and allies.

Thirty-one-year-old Hillary made quite an impression on Shipton, who was 12 years his senior. They made a strange pair, with the short, compact Shipton dwarfed by the towering, gangling Hillary, who had not yet gotten over his feelings of social inadequacy.

As they approached Mount Everest from the southwest, Shipton wanted to take a close look from a neighboring high peak. He chose 23,000-foot Pumori. On September 30, 1951, Shipton and Hillary climbed to about 20,000 feet on that mountain. Gazing northeast, they saw the immense floor that exists between Everest to the north, Lhotse to the south, and Nuptse to the southeast. This was the Western Cwm. Looking upward, they saw the South Col. In *High Adventure*, Hillary recalled the moment:

> Almost casually I looked toward the Western Cwm, although I didn't expect to see much of it from here. To my astonishment the whole valley lay revealed to our eyes. A long, narrow, snowy trough swept from the top of the icefall and climbed steeply up the face of Lhotse at the head of the Cwm. And even as the same thought was simmering in my own mind, Shipton said, 'There's a route there!'

This was more than they had expected, more than they had dared to hope. However difficult it was, a route existed, a means by which one could approach Mount Everest from the south.

The Icefall

When we think of the majestic Himalaya, we often forget the massive glaciers that snake their way through those mountains. The Khumbu Icefall lay between Nuptse (to the south), Lhotse (to the northeast) and Everest (dead straight north).

The Khumbu Icefall has claimed more lives than any other part of the South Col route to Everest. Located at 18,000 feet, the large towers of ice have been known to crack without warning, opening up large crevasses into which many people have fallen. Huge blocks of ice the size of cars or even houses tumble down the glacier from time to time, possibly crushing climbers who are in the way. Here, a mountaineer uses a ladder to bridge a gap.

Hillary, Shipton, and the others found the icefall tougher than expected.

Hillary led the way in the attack on the icefall. Day after day, he and the others picked their way around columns of ice and over crevasses. Each section earned a name, with Mike's Horror, Hillary's Horror, and the Ghastly Crevasse topping the list. After 10 days, Shipton called off the attack. Not only were more people needed, but the group needed better equipment, and, quite possibly, a series of ladders to make the icefall navigable for the Sherpa porters. There was one very tense moment when four men, including Hillary and Shipton, all slipped at once. Hillary served as the belay, or anchor, and everyone came off safe.

Shipton split his team into two groups, with he and Hillary forming one team. They explored the northeast of Mount Everest for some days, making a swing near Makalu before returning to base camp. Earle Riddiford and the other group, meanwhile, had done great things in the southwestern area of Mount Everest. The terrain was going to be a lot clearer to those who came the following year.

Had they arrived earlier in the season, the team might have made an attempt on Mount Everest, but winter was coming on and supplies were short. Shipton was famed for his ability to thrive on a low-calorie diet, but some expedition members did not have the same makeup. Therefore, that was all the team could accomplish that year.

Shipton and the British climbers went back to India, while Hillary and Riddiford took a rather dangerous route to Katmandu. On arriving there, the New Zealanders were greeted with great enthusiasm by the British embassy, but there was bad news. The Kingdom of Nepal had granted Switzerland not one, but two separate attempts to conquer Mount Everest in 1952. The British and New Zealanders would have to wait until 1953 for their attempt. As Hillary expressed it: "Our dream castles tumbled down merrily around our ears!"

Shipton wrote up his results in *The Mount Everest Reconnaissance Expedition*. Published in 1952, the book had some of the best photographs of Everest and its sister mountains ever seen, with much clearer markings of the different approaches. Shipton made much of the fact that the Western Cwm could lead, by way of the Lhotse Face, to the South Col. From there, it seemed it would be possible to make an attempt on the southwest ridge of Mount Everest. Shipton also emphasized the dangers:

> No experienced mountaineer can be optimistic about the challenges of finding his way up any great Himalayan peak. The vast scale on which these giants are built greatly increased the likelihood of the climber being faced by sheer impossibility—an unclimbable wall, slopes dominated by hanging glaciers, or avalanche-swept couloirs [French for "passage" or "corridor"].

Ed Hillary was well aware of the challenges but was still optimistic. The survey had been such a success that he believed 1952 would be the year Mount Everest would be conquered.

Cho Oyu

Hillary returned to New Zealand, where he recounted his adventures to an envious George Lowe, who had been left behind after Mukut Parbat. Hillary made it clear that he intended for Lowe to be included in any plans in 1952. The British–New Zealand climbers knew that the Swiss had two opportunities to take Mount Everest in 1952, but they were not going to be idle. Shipton was at it again, organizing an expedition to Cho Oyu, which was located about 20 miles west of Mount Everest.

Hillary still worked as a beekeeper, at least for half the year. He had few, if any, thoughts of fame or fortune. Rather, he was possessed of a great dream: to be the first person to stand atop Mount Everest.

Many other men had this dream before him, and this dream had led several of them to their deaths. Yet, this did not deter Hillary. He had seen the great Himalaya, had walked in the shadow of Mount Everest, and the mountain had become an all-consuming passion. Given that the Swiss had Mount

TENZING NORGAY

There have been conflicting accounts of the early life of Tenzing Norgay. One account is that he was a Sherpa born and brought up in Khumbu in Nepal. The most recent account states that he was born a Tibetan in the Kharta Valley in Tibet and was sold to work as a servant to a Sherpa family in Nepal.

His exact date of birth is unknown, but he knows it was late May by the weather and the crops. Born Namgyal Wangdi in 1914, he was the eleventh of thirteen children, most of whom died young. On the suggestion of a high lama, he changed his name to Tenzing Norgay (*Norgay* means "fortunate"), and he always believed he had good fortune. At the age of 18, Tenzing moved to Darjeeling, India, hoping to join one of the British expeditions to Mount Everest. At that time, because Nepal was closed to foreigners, climbers had begun using members of the large Sherpa population in Darjeeling as porters and guides. By 1935, Tenzing had managed to get hired on Eric Shipton's expedition. Based on the job he did there, he continued to get hired on subsequent climbs, including first ascents in India, Nepal, and Pakistan. Yet, Everest continued to be his main interest.

After World War II, Nepal opened its borders to foreigners at the same time that Tibet closed its northern route. Though he would work with many nationalities over the years, Tenzing clearly enjoyed the Swiss the most because they treated the Sherpas as equals. In 1952, Tenzing became the climbing partner of Raymond Lambert, a big hearted, flamboyant Swiss climber. During this climb, Tenzing and Lambert reached 28,250 feet but had to turn back. Their second attempt together also failed due to bad weather.

On May 29, 1953, Tenzing and Edmund Hillary became the first people known to reach the summit of Mount Everest. Hillary and Tenzing reached the top of the world, yet a controversy brewed for years over who was actually first to set his foot upon the summit. Both men, who remained

(Continues)

friends for their rest of their lives, continued to answer that they reached the top together, as a team. Tenzing and Hillary received many honors and were celebrated by world leaders and heads of state. Tenzing became the first field director of the Himalayan Mountaineering Institute, a position he held for 22 years. In 1978, he founded Tenzing Norgay Adventures. The trekking adventure company continues to be run by his son Jamling, who himself reached the summit of Everest in 1996.

Tenzing found it difficult adjusting to this new life of celebrity. A simple man, he became a political symbol, unwittingly involved in controversies he did not understand or care about. Tenzing died of a cerebral hemorrhage in 1986, at the age of 71. The procession that followed his funeral bier (a portable stand on which a coffin lies in state) was nearly a mile long.

Everest booked for 1952, Hillary and his mates would have to make do with another of the great mountains.

The passage was the same as before: Auckland to Australia, and then on to India. He joined Eric Shipton, Earle Riddiford, and three Englishmen in the spring of 1952.

The Cho Oyu expedition proved a failure, due largely to international conflict. Chinese troops had invaded Tibet and were in the neighborhood of the northern slopes of Cho Oyu. Naturally, Shipton was reluctant to involve his team in a dangerous international incident, so the all-out assault on Cho Oyu was called off and substituted by a limited three-man attempt with Hillary, Lowe, and Tom Bourdillon. Although there was an exciting moment in late May, when Hillary was at 22,500 feet, he had to pull back and the assault on Cho Oyu ended.

Bitterly disappointed, Hillary and Lowe asked Shipton for permission to explore one of the most dangerous mountain passes just west of Cho Oyu. With some time to spare, they made it, but a major storm blew up. Hillary and Lowe had a difficult time getting back through that pass and to the safety of the southern side of the Himalaya. Hillary was not very descriptive about the kinds of dangers he faced. Reading his account, one might think it was just another weekend's work. Then again, mountain climbing never seemed like work to him: It was sheer pleasure.

Rejoining Shipton and the others, Hillary and Lowe were delighted to learn that the Swiss team had come close but failed in its attempt to reach the summit of Mount Everest. Legendary Swiss climber Raymond Lambert and Sherpa Tenzing Norgay had reached 28,000 feet, but they found themselves stranded. They had to spend the night at that altitude with no sleeping bags, barely operable oxygen canisters, and no stove, producing only a trickle of drinking water by melting snow over a candle. The next morning they continued on, at times crawling on all fours, finally coming to a halt just 820 feet (250 meters) short of the summit. As they expressed it, they might have reached the top of Everest that day, but they surely would not have lived to tell the tale.

The British and New Zealanders were not out of the woods yet. The Swiss had been granted the privilege of making two assaults on Mount Everest, one in the late spring and the other in early autumn. But Hillary was much cheered to learn that it was possible that Great Britain and New Zealand would have the special opportunity in 1953.

Going
for the Gold

By the spring of 1953, millions of people around the globe wanted to see the conquest of Mount Everest. It had been almost a hundred years since Mount Everest, also known as Peak XV, had been surveyed and it was almost 30 years since Mallory and Irvine had been lost on the northern slope.

Leadership

Hillary received a letter from England on October 16, 1952. It read:

Dear Hillary,

I believe that Eric Shipton has written to tell you about the change in leadership of the 1953 Everest Expedition; you may, in any case, have seen press reports. I expect that you must be feeling puzzled and disappointed that this should have come to pass; it is most unfortunate that it should have happened in this way, and very bad luck on Eric Shipton.

Colonel John Hunt, a British army regular with mountain-climbing experience, went on to explain that Hunt, not Shipton, would be the leader of the British attempt on Everest in the spring of 1953. Would Hillary come?

Hillary learned that Shipton—his boyhood hero, and now his adult friend—had been cast aside by the Himalayan Club. There were several reasons.

Although Shipton was a terrific mountain climber and a fine leader, he was not given to organization. Some of his climbers from 1951 and 1952 had complained of the lack of supplies and the haphazard way some decisions were made. Hillary, however, always had the highest regard for Shipton. Still, the Himalayan Club had made its decision, and it was up to Hillary as to whether he would return to Everest.

Maybe not, was Hillary's first thought. But it did not take long for the thrill of mountaineering to overcome his resistance. By the end of the year, he was fully on board with the expedition and its new leader, John Hunt.

As usual, Rex Hillary agreed to manage the apiary in Ed's absence. Rex's wife also made a rather special cap for her brother-in-law: solid blue at the top and blue and white striped on the sides, it had a visor and a back flap (such as are used in the Sahara) to prevent his neck from being sun burned.

Ed Hillary and George Lowe were photographed as they left for the Himalaya. A handsomer, jauntier pair could hardly be imagined.

Full-on

Previous British attempts on Everest had been well staffed with climbers but lacking in sufficient supplies and organization. This was not the case with the 1953 group.

Shown are some of the British expedition that conquered Mount Everest in May 1953. Led by John Hunt, the group totaled more than 400 people, including 362 porters, 20 Sherpa guides, and 10,000 pounds of equipment. Hillary is fifth from the left in the back row, wearing the special striped cap made by his sister-in-law.

A military man, a fine climber, and a man possessed of a great desire, John Hunt spared no effort. He hired almost 400 Sherpas to bring the vast expedition supplies from Katmandu to the shadow of Mount Everest, and he conducted experiments with two systems of oxygen (closed circuit and open circuit) to give his climbers every possible chance.

There were two New Zealanders, two army officers, three medical doctors, three scientists, two schoolteachers, one travel agent, one photographer, and one beekeeper among them, making this one of the most diverse, interesting groups of explorers yet seen. Everyone gathered in Katmandu, Nepal's capital, in March 1953.

Tension

Although the explorers and their 400 porters worked together well, they were not without troubles in the early days. Tenzing Norgay described some of the difficulties in his autobiography, *Tiger of the Snows*. For example, the British and New Zealand climbers were housed at the British Embassy, while the Sherpas were given a barn in which to live: one that had no bathrooms. Upset by this, many of the Sherpas relieved themselves on the road in front of the embassy, leading to the first reprimand issued by John Hunt.

Because of his experience, Tenzing Norgay was named *sirdar* of the expedition—meaning it was his task to round up, direct, and conduct the porters. He was caught between the European-style professionalism of John Hunt—who expected quick obedience to any order—and the Asiatic-style of camaraderie of his fellow Sherpas. Tenzing's life would reflect this push and pull, sometimes with harsh consequences. Still, nearly everyone on the expedition marveled at his ability to remain levelheaded and cheerful in all circumstances.

Among the 11 climbers there was little tension but some competition. While Hillary and George Lowe, who were an old climbing team now, hoped to be the "assault" group, John Hunt did not want a British expedition to be overshadowed in the headlines by the accomplishments of two New Zealanders. Therefore, a Hillary-Lowe team was out of the question. Meanwhile, other climbers hoped for their moment of glory. No one was certain who would have the honor of making the grand attempt; that was up to Hunt, and he did not reveal his hand until late in the expedition.

Thyangboche

Leaving Katmandu, the entire expedition slowly marched through the gorgeous Nepalese countryside. Spring was in full bloom, and the land was rich in plant growth. Hillary later remembered that they ate enormous meals along the way to counteract the likelihood of deprivation and fatigue that may come later. By the time they reached the monastery of Thyangboche—where every Everest expedition had gone to be blessed by the lama and monks—the climbers appreciated Hunt's method. A man of science, he was well versed in the theory of acclimatization, meaning that one must slowly acclimate to the rigors of high altitude. The slower the better.

While at Thyangboche, the high lama blessed the expedition but also expressed doubt that Everest could be conquered. There were conversations about the yeti (also known as the Abominable Snowman), talks that led Hillary to think about future explorations. Nonetheless, by early April, the expedition had packed up and headed for the king of all mountains, the golden prize, Everest itself.

The Icefall

The expedition moved in three stages. Hillary had the honor of leading the first group, and they reached the icefall in mid-April 1953. To his surprise and horror, it was much harsher than he remembered from two years earlier. The Khumbu Glacier, which twists its way down the southern slopes of Everest, had changed its path, creating even more destruction than before.

In *View from the Summit*, Hillary described one of the dangerous scenes from the icefall area: "George Lowe was in the lead as we approached it. When he came to the first crevasse he stopped and eyed it with obvious dislike. 'You didn't cross this bridge did you, Ed?' he shouted back. I assured him that this was the way we had gone."

Lowe put his ice axe on the edge of the ice bridge, and, before he could take a single swing, it fell out of sight. He and Hillary went more cautiously from then on.

Days passed and Hillary and his group navigated their way through the icefall. They were accustomed to it now and believed they could go back and forth without too much danger,

GLOBAL WARMING—GLOBAL COOLING

In the twenty-first century, most scientists and public persons are concerned about the dangers of global warming. Records indicate that, across the globe, the average mean temperature increased by a full degree Fahrenheit between 1900 and the present. In the 1950s, the decade of Hillary's most impressive mountain climbing, global *cooling* seemed more likely.

Even the best scientists admit they cannot be certain about the cause of climate change. Studies do show, however, that much of the global warming of 1860–2010 coincided with an increase in use of fossil fuels. These fossil fuels release carbon into the atmosphere, creating the so-called "greenhouse effect." Even so, the climate change has gone in cycles. For example:

The 1950s were a moderately cool decade;
The 1960s were, far and away, the coldest decade of the twentieth century;
The late 1980s showed a marked trend toward increasing warmth;
The 1990s showed a powerful acceleration of that warmth.

Global climate change has had adverse effects on the Himalaya and, therefore, upon mountain climbing. In the 1950s, when Hillary, Tenzing, and their team assaulted Everest, the Khumbu Glacier was very solid, leading to a difficult climb in the icefall area. Climbers who arrived a decade later had it even harder, as the cold weather of the 1960s led to increased ice. Since about 1975, however, it has become markedly easier to approach Everest, because the amount of ice has decreased due to the increasingly warm temperatures.

but it was completely different for the heavily laden Sherpas, without whom the entire expedition would fail. Just as Hillary was beginning to feel some confidence with the area, he learned that Hunt and the expedition's main body were only a day off. Hillary had hoped to have longer to solve the riddles posed by the icefall.

The Western Cwm

Viewed from the air or by satellite photograph, the Western Cwm stands out as one of the most forbidding and lonely of all Himalayan regions. The cwm is the floor that exists between Everest to the north, Lhotse to the south, and Nuptse to the southwest. One can see the Khumbu Glacier snaking its way between the three great mountains, making the region almost inaccessible.

This is where Hunt's organizational skills became fully apparent. While earlier British expeditions had come this far—including Shipton's in 1951—none had arrived with enough supplies and equipment to sustain a major assault on the mountain itself. Hunt stayed up late almost every night, the click-clack of his typewriter making an eerie sound in the darkness. Continually, he organized, then reorganized.

By now, Hillary had become more aware of Tenzing Norgay's climbing abilities. The two did not become close friends—at least not then—but they saw that they made an excellent climbing team. Hillary was about five inches taller than Tenzing, who was considerably fleshier, and this difference helped make them good at their respective jobs. Hillary often led—not always—and Tenzing proved an excellent belay man, reaching Hillary with his quick reflexes (the belayer controls the rope so that a falling climber does not fall very far). It is uncertain whether Hunt decided on his own or whether Hillary prompted him, but by the time the expedition started working on the Lhotse Face, Hillary and Tenzing had become a team.

Lhotse Face

Towering at 27,940 feet (8,516 meters), Lhotse is the world's fourth-highest mountain. Lhotse stands right in the path of would-be climbers of Everest; they cannot get around Lhotse but must go nearly to its summit to reach a place called the South Col. This became one of the most trying parts of the 1953 expedition.

Hillary, Tenzing, and Hunt were in a tent on the Western Cwm, looking up as Tom Bourdillon and Charles Evans worked their way up the Lhotse Face. This was not the climb of an hour, or even a day, but of nearly a week, and there were plenty of setbacks. The desire was to place Camp VII high on the Lhotse Face and get over to the Southern Col, but the going was very slow.

One day, Hillary and Tenzing looked up to see that Bourdillon and Evans had started but that their Sherpas had not moved from the tents. Now was the time, Hillary said. He and Tenzing were needed up on the Lhotse Face!

Hunt was not pleased with this development. By now, he had announced that there would be two assault teams, with Lowe and Bourdillon going first and Hillary and Tenzing second. He wanted Hillary and Tenzing to stay on the Western Cwm to get some needed rest. But he saw that Hillary was right; the Sherpas were not moving. So he gave the "yes," and the new team of Hillary and Tenzing went up the Lhotse Face.

This was one of the toughest challenges of the entire expedition. Hillary and Tenzing moved well, partly because of their similar climbing style and partly because of the open-circuit oxygen tanks they used. By afternoon, they had reached Camp VII of the Lhotse Face, and the mere presence of Tenzing was enough to get some of the Sherpas moving again.

The Southern Col

Years later, Tenzing wrote in *Tiger of the Snows*, "I think the Southern Col must be the loneliest place in the whole world."

So it seemed to Hillary, Tenzing, Evans, Bourdillon, and Hunt, all of whom crammed into two small tents on the Southern Col on the night of May 26–27, 1953. The wind was indescribably loud, and it seemed to get stronger as the night went on. Everyone seemed in reasonably good spirits, but there were private moments when even Hillary wondered why he had ever thought this a possibility. He was in the very teeth of the Everest-Lhotse-Nuptse combination.

On the morning of May 27, Hillary and Tenzing purposely stayed back, while Evans and Bourdillon made a daring move up Everest's southeast ridge. Meanwhile, Hunt and a Sherpa had a special job of their own: getting supplies, oxygen particularly, to a high level on the ridge in case a second assault was required. Hillary, Tenzing, and Lowe spent most of the day arranging things at Camp VIII, but they took moments out for furtive looks up the mountain. On one remarkable occasion the sky cleared just enough for them to make out Evans and Bourdillon on the south ridge and going strong.

"I noticed that Tenzing looked decidedly subdued," Hillary wrote. Only later did he realize the reason: If Evans and Bourdillon succeeded, there would not be a Sherpa in the first team to reach the top of Mount Everest.

Late in the afternoon, Hunt and the Sherpa returned. To say they were exhausted is a serious understatement: They were truly done in. The two had made a heroic effort to reach the neighborhood of 28,000 feet to dump supplies that now awaited the second assault team, if it was needed.

Still later, Evans and Bourdillon returned. They looked unreal, entirely covered in ice and so exhausted they had to be dragged to the campsite. What a tale they had to tell!

From the start, the two had experienced difficulties with their oxygen tanks, but they had continued to plow their way up the southwest ridge, where they had climbed higher than anyone had ever gone. They had actually stood on the South Summit (350 feet shy of the summit itself), torn about what to do. Bourdillon wished to continue, but Evans talked him out of it. Just as with the experience of Raymond Lambert and Tenzing Norgay a year earlier, they could have reached the summit but might not have lived to return to tell the story.

Everest remained unconquered.

Camp IX

On the morning of May 28, Hillary and Tenzing roped up for what they anticipated would be a big day. They watched nervously as an exhausted John Hunt and three others went down the slope, headed for the Western Cwm. Then Tenzing and Hillary—as well as George Lowe and Alfred Gregory and the Sherpa Ang Nyima—headed up the southwest ridge.

Hillary had trouble deciding what to bring along. All of the climbers felt overburdened, but there were some things he felt he could not do without. These included apricots and other sweets that proved essential to maintaining his morale. All morning they climbed, and by early afternoon they had reached the staggering height of 27,900 feet, not the highest men had ever gone, but certainly the highest yet for Hillary.

George Lowe, Alfred Gregory, and Ang Nyima left, heading back to Camp VIII. At Camp IX, Hillary and Tenzing looked at each other, realizing at the same time that this would be no easy night. They had a ledge, but it was so narrow that the tent had to sprawl across two parts, and when they had tightened down all the ropes and fastenings, there was barely enough room in there for the both of them.

The night before attempting the summit, Hillary and Tenzing camped out on a narrow ledge at Camp IX (now Camp IV) where there was barely enough room for the both of them. They slept at 27,900 feet, the highest anyone had ever camped. These very basic campsites are used during mountain climbers' ascents and descents. Here, yellow tents dot the landscape of Camp III on the Lhotse Face (Camp VII in 1953).

Hillary slept on the slightly higher section, with his long legs dangled across Tenzing's. Both men praised the open-circuit oxygen, which would give them a few hours of needed rest.

They closed their eyes and went to sleep.

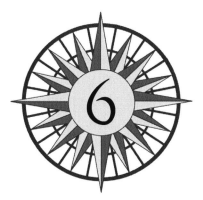

To the Top

Hillary and Tenzing awoke early on the morning of May 29, 1953. Their first feeling was one of amazement, both at the height at which they had slept and at the prospect of a fine day, which should have little wind. Within two hours, they had thawed Hillary's boots, wrapped Tenzing's four flags around the handle of his ice axe, and were ready to go.

South Summit

Up they went, up into the clouds. Of course they were concentrating on their feet and the positions of their bodies, but they were also conscious of lifting more, all the time. According to Hillary in *View from the Summit*:

> Towering over our heads was the South Summit and running along from it to the right were the great menacing cornices of the Kangshung Face. Ahead of me was a sharp narrow ridge, icy on the right and looking more manageable on the left.

Tenzing led at first, but Hillary then took over. They gained confidence the higher they went. The 30-pound cylinders of oxygen weighed heavily on their backs, but they knew that this oxygen was vital to their reaching the top. By 10 A.M., they had reached the South Summit, equaling the effort made by Bourdillon and Evans just two days earlier. Hillary continues his account in *View from the Summit*:

> We had a drink out of Tenzing's water bottle and I checked our oxygen supplies. Each of us had a bottle that was almost empty so, to save weight, we removed these and I attached our other full bottles firmly in place. It meant we had a total endurance of just under four hours.

It was now the final assault, the last 350 feet.

Top of the World

Sometime between 10 and 11 that morning, Hillary and Tenzing encountered a jutting piece of rock that completely blocked their path. They knew a little about it, from aerial photographs, but it proved even more formidable than they had feared. Measuring almost 40 feet (12 meters) high, this final rock slab prevented them from going anywhere. Had they come all this way only to fail?

Mallory and Irvine had failed. Eric Shipton, for all his skill, had never come this far. Evans and Bourdillon had been forced to turn back.

Hillary and Tenzing were not immortal. They were a first-rate climbing team, but they could be defeated. Yet, three things enabled them to succeed: the use of oxygen, the lack of wind that day, and their formidable willpower.

Hillary found a way under and through the terrible rock slab, which has since been named Hillary Step, and as he later put it, he hauled Tenzing up after him (conflicting reports of who hauled whom would dog the expedition members for many years). Minutes later, they stood on the very summit, the top of Mount Everest—one might say, the very top of the world.

It was 11:30 A.M. on March 29, 1953. In typical Anglo-Saxon fashion I stretched out my arm for a handshake

This photograph, taken by Edmund Hillary, shows Tenzing Norgay on the summit holding flags representing Great Britain, Nepal, India, and the United Nations. The two men hugged each other with joy and relief but could only stay on the summit for 15 minutes.

but this was not enough for Tenzing who threw his arms around my shoulders in a mighty hug and I hugged him back in return. With a feeling of mild surprise I realized that Tenzing was perhaps more excited at our success than I was.

Time was short. The limited oxygen supply meant they could only remain there for a brief amount of time. Still, in those minutes (about 15), Hillary and Tenzing did everything possible to celebrate their achievement. First, Hillary took a photograph of Tenzing. Clad almost entirely in black, and shrouded by his hood, Tenzing looks barely recognizable, but his axe handle proudly displays the four flags of Great Britain, India, Nepal, and the United Nations.

A devout Buddhist, Tenzing had brought a food offering, which he buried in the snow. Hillary did likewise, burying a small crucifix given to him by John Hunt. Hillary took a number of photographs, most of which later came out with astonishing clarity. Anyone who knew Mount Everest's topography and the geography of its neighbors would instantly be convinced that these photographs could only have been taken from one place: the very summit. Hillary thought of earlier expeditions:

> It was a sobering thought to remember how often these men had reached 28,000 feet without the benefits of our modern equipment and reasonably efficient oxygen sets. Inevitably, my thoughts turned to Mallory and Irvine who had lost their lives on this mountain thirty years before. With little hope I looked around for some sign that they had reached the summit, but could see nothing.

The Return

After 15 minutes, Hillary and Tenzing turned on their oxygen sets and began the long descent. They were quite aware that many a mountaineer had scaled a peak successfully only to perish on the return, so they went as slowly as they dared (they were fighting a balance between the need for care and the diminished amount of oxygen). They passed through the area now known as Hillary Step, and within an hour they reached the South Summit. Here the views were less spectacular, but there was a growing feeling of safety.

They continued down. Before long, they were at Camp IX, where they had spent the previous night. Hillary and Tenzing were delighted to unload some of their burdens to exchange them for new ones, but there was a growing elation within them. Not only had they reached the top, but they believed they would live to tell the tale!

Down, down they went, and in the midafternoon they reached the South Col. The day was still spectacular—cold but without wind—and as they looked back up at the peaks, Hillary and Tenzing doubtless had a feeling of astonishment: Had they really gone all that way? Minutes later they were greeted by Hillary's old friend George Lowe.

Queen and Commonwealth

On May 31, Hillary and Tenzing came down to Camp VI, where an anxious John Hunt met them. Had they done it?

Yes, they had, and they had all the pictures to prove it.

Hunt had been a tough leader on this expedition, but his toughness had proved to be worth it. As demanding of himself as he was of his team, Hunt had led the effort, and the success was as much his as it was Hillary and Tenzing's. Expedition member Jan Morris hurried down through the icefall to Base Camp, hoping to get a special message off to the London *Times*.

Morris moved with great speed and sent a cabled message to Katmandu. From there, it was relayed to London and the *Times* had the scoop. On June 2, 1953, the morning of the

John Hunt, Edmund Hillary, and Tenzing Norgay became instantly famous, receiving medals and other honors throughout their lives. They used their money and prestige to aid various causes for the poor. Here, they receive medals from the president of India after their successful Mount Everest expedition.

coronation of England's Queen Elizabeth II, the *Times* broke the news that two climbers—a New Zealander and a Nepalese Sherpa—had reached Mount Everest's summit. To the throngs that greeted Queen Elizabeth II on her big day, it was as if a second queen was about to inaugurate a golden age of exploration and discovery, much as Queen Elizabeth the First had done in her reign (1558–1603).

At the center of it all were three men: John Hunt, Tenzing Norgay, and Ed Hillary.

Glory and Conflict

The entire Everest expedition team returned first to Base Camp, and then to Katmandu, where the media began peppering them with questions: Who was first on top of the mountain? Who deserved greater praise?

Hillary and Tenzing had become good friends by this point, but the language difference between them—English and Sherpa—made communication difficult. Neither Hillary nor Tenzing appreciated the question of who had gone first: They both thought it an unnecessary distraction. Yet, the media of England, India, and even Nepal were persistent, insisting on knowing which of the men had the right to the glory. There were annoying cartoons, such as a Nepalese one that showed a cheerful, fit Tenzing hauling an exhausted Hillary to the summit. Photographs taken at press conferences in Nepal and India clearly show the strain, with Hunt, Hillary, and Tenzing often assuming grim expressions. If this was fame, it certainly had its downside.

By then, Hillary had learned of his knighthood. Queen Elizabeth II had honored him as Sir Edmund Hillary and had honored Colonel John Hunt as Sir John Hunt (both men later became Knights of the Garter). No one seems to have considered Tenzing for a knighthood. He had to make do with an Order of the British Commonwealth. Still, all three men had been vaulted from relative obscurity to star status, and it seemed that all of them would be set for life, at least financially.

A little more than a month after leaving Everest, Hillary flew to England for his second visit to Great Britain (his first had been in the spring of 1950). He met Queen Elizabeth, heard the roar of the crowd outside Westminster Abbey, and realized—with some surprise—that they were cheering for him.

From there it was on to New York City and a triumphal reception there. Finally, he went home to Auckland, where, predictably, his father treated him very much the same as always.

WHO WAS FIRST?

Does it matter? This is a question often asked in the twenty-first century, a time when people are bombarded with the intimate details of celebrity life. But in the mid-twentieth century, when Hillary and Tenzing went up Mount Everest, it mattered very much indeed.

England was proud to have Ed Hillary represent the commonwealth on the mountain, but it hurt a little that there was no native-born son in the final assault party. India and Nepal both claimed Tenzing as a native son, and sometimes it seemed they would fight each other over who got the glory. The United States had no one in the 1953 expedition. Switzerland—proud of its long tradition of mountain climbing—had failed in 1952. So, countries were unrelenting in their demands to know who was first.

Hillary and Tenzing were initially embarrassed, then put off, by the relentless questions of the newspaper people. Eventually, they released a statement that claimed they had reached the top at almost the same time. Of course, that satisfied no one, and the question continued: Had the Kiwi or the Sherpa been the first man on the summit? Here is how Tenzing described it in his autobiography, *Tiger of the Snows*:

> A little below the summit Hillary and I stopped. We looked up. Then we went on. The rope that joined us was thirty feet long, but I held most of it in loops in my hands so that there was only about six feet between us. I was not thinking of first and second. I did not say to myself, 'There is a golden apple up there. I will push Hillary and run for it.' We went on slowly, steadily. And then we were there. Hillary stepped on top first. And I stepped up after him.

Finding Love

Hillary had not experienced much luck with women. When he was a student, a high school gymnastics teacher had taunted him about his size and appearance, leading Hillary to believe girls would not be interested in him. Years before his Everest climb there had been a brief love affair in his early twenties, but there had been no romantic involvement since. Now, as the co-conqueror of Mount Everest, he could expect to be pursued by many marriageable women. Luckily, he had fastened his attention on one before he attained fame. She was Louise Rose of Auckland.

Ed and Louise married in Auckland on September 15, 1953. George Lowe served as Hillary's best man. Years later, Hillary described marrying Louise as one of the most solid decisions of his life, for the two complemented each other. His serious, sometimes obsessive desire to reach goals was tempered by her outgoing, vivacious nature. Marriage did not slow him down in any way. Louise was soon resigned to the idea of being a grass widow (a wife whose husband will return after a limited time away, usually after a voyage) six months out of the year.

Happiness seemed complete for the Kiwi who did not take himself too seriously. He was still a young man, a bit shy of 34.

The Pole

WHEN ED AND LOUISE RETURNED FROM THEIR AMERICAN speaking tour, it was still in doubt as to whether he would go to the Himalayas again. What, after all, did he have to prove?

For the first time in his 34 years, Hillary was ready to settle down. He had found happiness with Louise, and there was no need to worry about money. Hillary actually considered settling back into the beekeeping business. He suffered from guilt that his brother, Rex, had gone to such lengths to keep the family business going. Nonetheless, when Hillary was offered the opportunity to serve for the first time as leader of a Himalayan expedition, he could not resist.

Mount Makalu

In the spring of 1954, Hillary, three members of the 1953 team, and a number of others trekked up into the Himalaya. Their objective was Mount Makalu (27,766 feet/8,463 meters), which had never been climbed.

Hillary had much more responsibility than in the past. It was his task to assign climbing rotations, to ensure that there were ample supplies, and to incorporate new methods (including new types of oxygen) into the expedition. In all of this, he proved quite able and competent, but the expedition experienced grief just the same.

At about 20,000 feet, one climber fell into a terrible crevasse. Hillary and another climber stood 30 feet above him, looking anxiously into the hole. Dusk was coming on, and all they could do was throw sleeping bags down into the hole and beg their companion to get into them. Unfortunately, he was unable to because his broken limbs prevented it.

When morning came, Hillary and the others were right on the scene. Hillary attempted a rescue, going down by rope. He placed the rope near his chest rather than his thighs and suffered broken ribs as a result. Finally, they managed to extricate their team member and, over the next three days, brought him down to lesser altitudes. He lost several fingers and a foot as a result of frostbite.

Although the injury had sobered Hillary and the others a good deal, they were not discouraged and desired to push on. The result was disaster. For the first time, at 21,000 feet, Hillary suffered high-altitude, or mountain, sickness due to the strain of the expedition and his cracked ribs. High-altitude sickness can occur when someone who normally lives at lower altitudes goes to an altitude above 8,000 feet, where there is less oxygen. Some of the most common symptoms include headache, fatigue, stomach illness, shortness of breath, dizziness, and sleep disturbance. Extreme cases can be fatal.

Now it was Hillary who had to be carried down a set of narrow slopes. International media kept a close watch on the expedition. In London, Sir John Hunt was asked to write an obituary for Hillary just in case the worst should occur. Hillary's powers of recuperation proved as good as ever, and he soon appeared hale and hearty. His illness was quite a setback for him, however, and he knew that his future as a climber was compromised. Once a person experiences high-altitude sickness, he may continue having a difficult time at those heights.

Family Life

Hillary returned to New Zealand, where he and Louise now lived in a splendid Auckland location. Her parents had sold them the land, and they commissioned a first-rate builder to create the home of their dreams. Their first child, Peter, was born in 1954.

Louise would have preferred a husband who was home and settled, but she came to accept this was not the case. When asked by the media about future expeditions, she replied that she thought he should go on them. Still, they had a happy home life, adding to the family daughters Sarah (1955) and Belinda (1959).

Antarctica

New Zealand wished to be part of the International Geophysical Year (IGY), a global program of geophysical research, which ran from July 1, 1957, until December 31, 1958. This ambitious undertaking was created and sponsored by scientists from around the globe who wished to understand the world better, and part of the effort was directed toward Antarctica.

In England, the idea was put forth for a major expedition to cross the frozen continent, something attempted by Edmund Scott in 1901 and Ernest Shackelton in 1913. Leadership of the 1957–1958 expedition was given to Vivian Ernest Fuchs (later Sir Vivian Fuchs), who was also known as "Bunny." Bunny was born on the Isle of Wight, off England's southern coast, in 1908. A geologist by profession, Bunny stood at more than six feet tall and was considered a natural leader. He knew Antarctica as well as anyone, having made a crossing with dog sleds and vehicles in 1949–1950.

Although Edmund Hillary married and had three children, he continued to travel with the support of his wife, Louise. In order to spend more time together, his family began to travel with him. While en route to join Hillary in a village in Nepal, where he was helping to build a hospital, Louise and daughter Belinda were killed in a plane crash. He mourned their deaths for many years.

In 1956, Fuchs and Hillary met in England to plan the expedition. They agreed that Fuchs would be the leader, while Hillary would lead a secondary team. Fuchs's British team would travel from Shackleton Base on the Weddell Sea to the

HEROIC AGE OF ANTARCTIC EXPLORATION

Before 1800, very little was known about Antarctica. The British initiated the age of polar exploration in the 1890s, with the Royal Geographical Society sponsoring expeditions to the Southern Hemisphere. This age reached its peak with Robert Falcon Scott's two expeditions, in 1901–1904 and 1910–1913, respectively. On the second occasion, Scott reached the South Pole only to receive the news that a Norwegian expedition, led by Roald Amundsen, had beaten him there by five weeks. Scott and his four companions all died on the return trek from exhaustion, hunger, and exposure to the extreme cold, and many people blamed Amundsen. Amundsen had kept his planned expedition a secret, although he knew other missions were being planned at the time. In recent years, biographers have seen Scott as less than heroic, incompetent even. Both views tend to be extreme.

Most famous of all were the expeditions of Ernest Shackleton. Charismatic and beloved by his team, Shackleton wanted to lead the first expedition across Antarctica. He failed, but it was a glorious failure, with books and magazine articles being written about him to this day and a T.V. movie, *Shackleton*.

The heroic age faded in the 1920s, largely because of the appearance of new equipment. Explorers now had ships with radar, icebreakers, and planes. Despite all these advances, getting to the South Pole remains a formidable task.

U.S. station at the South Pole and from there to the coast, where Hillary's team should have already surveyed and provided the site with supplies. Hillary's team would also serve as backup in case of an emergency. The New Zealand team would establish another base (Scott Base on the Ross Sea) on the other side of Antarctica, where the journey was to end.

Weddell Sea

Hillary sailed south with Fuchs and the British expedition. Though he had seen much of the world by now, Hillary had never sailed in the South Atlantic. The rough waters there won his wholehearted admiration. The British team disembarked in the Weddell Sea, but there were difficulties right from the start.

The ship nearly broke in the ice. The tractors were landed in slushy areas. It proved impossible to locate the right materials in the ship's hold. None of this detracted from Fuchs's leadership qualities. The accomplishments and survival of the advance party say a lot about the skill of Fuchs and his men. Hillary learned from these mistakes. By the time he returned to England and then journeyed home to New Zealand, Hillary had devised all sorts of plans to ensure that his team did not encounter the same difficulties.

The Ross Ice Shelf

In the autumn of 1956, Hillary collected his team in New Zealand. Harry Ayres, Hillary's first mentor, who had never had a chance in the Himalaya, was part of the group. Before leaving, the expedition members met Prince Philip, the Duke of Edinburgh, aboard his private yacht.

To songs of Christmastime and Old England, the men of New Zealand sailed south. Hillary had done his work well, but naturally there were things he could not foresee. The expedition disembarked at the Ross Ice Shelf but needed to locate a better place for the base, a little to the northwest. He was helped enormously by the presence of a U.S. ship, headed by Admiral George Dufek. Among their many accomplishments, Dufek and his team established bases on Ross Island and were the first Americans to set foot at the South Pole.

Scott Base

Hillary and company—he and three others began calling themselves the "Old Firm"—wintered at Scott Base in McMurdo Sound. The aluminum sheets they brought worked well for the creation of temporary shelters, but there were plenty of challenges during the long winter months. Only with the change of season, and the arrival of 24-hour daylight, did they set out on their mission.

Hillary and his team left in October 1957, heading straight south. They ran into trouble almost from the very beginning. Sometimes the ice was too thick and they had to go around these spots. More often they encountered soft snow in which the tractors bogged down. On three separate occasions, they ran into terrible crevasses that threatened to swallow the tractors. Whatever the reason, they made only six and a half miles the first day but then accelerated to 23 miles on the second day.

Usually, Hillary drove in the lead tractor. He and his fellows discovered that the Ferguson tractors were rugged enough for this kind of work, but they provided few comforts. There was a windshield of sorts but no roof, and the team often drove in temperatures of minus 20—even minus 30—degrees Celsius.

A few days of good weather followed, in which the team made good progress. There was a 30-mile day, followed by 32 miles, and another day in which they traveled 58 miles. They often drove by night, although that was not a problem: In Antarctica at this time of year, there were 24 hours of daylight.

At Skelton Depot, on Skelton Glacier, they met a dog team led by Harry Ayres. The dogs were quite valuable as scouts, for Ayres could radio back to the tractors, informing them of weather and ice conditions ahead. On one bad occasion, Hillary and the tractor team went past the dog team in a bad storm, then had to spend almost two days looking for them.

From 1955–1958, Hillary led the New Zealand section of the Trans-Antarctic Expedition. On January 4, 1958, he participated in the first successful overland expedition to the South Pole since Robert F. Scott's expedition in 1912. Here, members of the team sit on top of a tractor pulling wood through the snow.

Eventually the team reached Plateau Depot, where they deposited several large, 350-pound drums of fuel for Fuchs's team. At this point, Hillary wrote of himself: "slightly crazy, frequently terrified and not a bad navigator—that about summed it up." The craze came from the amount of responsibilities he faced. The terror usually centered on the fear of a tractor falling into a crevasse. His summation of not being a bad navigator referred to the many hours he spent working with an astro-compass to determine their position.

Then everything began to fall apart.

Team member Murray Ellis suffered a recurrence of an old back injury, and Peter Mulgrew fell onto a tractor he was working on. Both men had to be evacuated by air. Hillary then came down with a very bad case of the flu and sometimes would be found wandering around the campsite with a dazed expression. Hillary had sent a message to Fuchs offering to "scrub the southward jaunt" if Fuchs thought Hillary's team could be of use elsewhere. Hillary received a response to "go ahead." To complicate matters, according to Fuchs's original plans and the Ross Sea Committee, which was in charge of Hillary's team, Hillary was to turn back to Scott Base or remain in the depot to ensure that it was found by Fuchs.

Those words led to one of the biggest mix-ups of Hillary's career. When he first agreed to undertake this mission, he had known it was Fuchs's to lead and that the New Zealanders would play a supporting role. Hillary and Fuchs had been in very tentative contact for a few weeks, however, having been forced to communicate using Morse code relayed by five separate transmissions. In addition, some of the New Zealanders were starting to feel a keen rivalry with their British counterparts. Hillary and his group had moved with such speed that if they simply waited for Fuchs, it would mean days, perhaps weeks, of just sitting around, which they were not prepared to do.

Hillary waited for Murray Ellis and Peter Mulgrew to rejoin the expedition and then left six large drums of fuel at what he called Midway Depot. On December 10, 1957, he and his team set out for the South Pole. Sixteen days later, Hillary sent a special message to London: "Am hellbent for the Pole, God willing and crevasses permitting."

One Last Holdup

Although Fuchs was not completely aware of Hillary's dash for the pole, he was getting nervous. His Sno-Cats—truck-sized vehicles with tracks used to travel in snow—were bigger and stronger than Hillary's Ferguson tractors. Still, they were encountering troubles in the ice; the men were 1,200 miles away from Hillary's team, and Fuchs thought he might soon be low on petrol. He sent an urgent message to Hillary asking him to remain at the fuel depot and to be ready to provide on-the-spot assistance. Not only did Hillary decline to pull back, he suggested Fuchs and his team wait to be evacuated by American aircraft: They could always start again the following year.

To make matters worse, officials in London declared to the media that there was no race for the pole—before anyone had said there was. Immediately a controversy blew up. Was Hillary trying to steal Fuchs's glory?

Hillary and company were unaware of the controversy brewing. They pushed on. At 12:30 P.M. on January 4, 1958, they pulled into the Scott-Amundsen Station at the South Pole, which had been established by Admiral Dufek the previous year. Hillary's radio man sent a one-word message to Scott Base—Rhubarb—which was reported back to Great Britain, New Zealand, and then the rest of the world. Hillary and his New Zealanders had done it.

LinkUp

Hillary and his team rested for several days before flying back on February 7 to the South Pole to rendezvous with Fuchs. With the race-for-the-pole controversy still raging, how would Fuchs react? Hillary reports in *View from the Summit*:

> "Bunny jumped out of the leading Sno-Cat and we shook hands and exchanged a warm greeting. I don't know how Bunny really felt but I was mighty pleased to see him. I had no desire to spend another winter in Antarctica."

The entire team, Brits and New Zealanders, traveled several hundred miles through crevassed areas to reach Scott Base in Antarctica. Later, both men made it clear there had been no race. Though Hillary's team had certainly moved faster and more efficiently, Bunny Fuchs did achieve his dream: He and his team crossed all of Antarctica in fewer than 100 days.

Hillary politely declined an invitation to travel to London and give talks with Fuchs. Hillary had seen neither Louise nor his children in more than 16 months!

Joy and Sorrow

TOWARD THE END OF HIS LONG LIFE, HILLARY OFTEN REFLECTED on what a lucky fellow he had been. There was truth in the words, to be sure, but he also had his share of tragedy.

Building Schools in the Himalaya

Hillary had thought that once he reached the heights of Mount Everest that he was done with the Himalaya, but the opposite was true: He was only beginning. In the early 1960s, he asked a local Sherpa what was needed to improve his life and that of the Sherpa community. The answer, quoted in Greg Mortensen and David Oliver Relin's *Three Cups of Tea*, went like this:

> With all respect, Sahib [term of respect for "sir" or "friend"], you have little to teach us in strength and toughness. And we don't envy you your restless spirits. Perhaps we are happier than you? But we would like our children to go to school. Of all the things you have, learning is the one we most desire for our children.

Typically, Hillary went to work. He set up a nonprofit organization called the Himalayan Trust to improve the living conditions of the people in the Himalayas.

The First School

Bringing builders to the Himalaya was difficult enough, but transporting the material was even tougher. There were almost no factories in eastern Nepal and very little raw material to use. The Sherpas had become adept, over centuries, at building houses in combinations of wood and stone, but material conservation was always high on their list. As he worked to raise funds and collect materials, Hillary also began to have his first worries about conservation in the Everest region. When he and Tenzing reached the summit in 1953, there was minimal evidence of the effects of man in the region. Just a decade later, climbers could find the waste dumps from earlier expeditions—including theirs from 1953.

Hillary and his group decided that aluminum was the toughest, most resilient material for building in the mountains. The aluminum came all the way from New Zealand and was then carried by hundreds of Sherpa porters. There was plenty of exhausting work, but there was also a great satisfaction when things began coming together. Hillary drove plenty of nails and screws in the final stages, and he had the immense delight of being present for the dedication of the new school by the lama of Thyangboche. Now, just 10 years after his great climb, Hillary was starting to feel more complete with his life. He and Louise now had three children—Peter, Sarah, and Belinda. They had a wonderful home in New Zealand and terrific friends in many parts of the world. The Hillarys spent a full year in Chicago while Ed traveled and lectured for the World Book Corporation, which became a major sponsor for his building of schools in the Himalaya.

Hillary felt a deep obligation to the Nepalese people who helped him, and he spent the rest of his life helping them. In 1960 he created the Himalayan Trust, a nonprofit organization that helps to improve the lives of Sherpa communities in Nepal. It has since been responsible for building more than 30 schools, 2 hospitals, 12 medical clinics, 3 airfields, and many bridges and fresh-water pipelines. Here, a Sherpa boy presents Hillary with a petition for a school.

More and Better

Hillary was building more schools, and soon he was thinking about building hospitals. He found a right-hand man in his brother.

Rex had built his own house from scratch, without any training, and had gained confidence in his own abilities as a carpenter over the years. By the late 1960s, he had partnered with his elder brother, leading and supervising the building of schools in Nepal. Not just Rex but the entire Hillary family was involved. Louise came to love the Himalaya, though she was never that interested in climbing, and the three Hillary children came to know the Solo Khumbu almost as well as Auckland. Still, there was heartbreak over the years.

Losing His Parents

Hillary lost both his parents in 1965. Little is known of the circumstances of his father's death; father and son do not appear to have drawn closer in Percival's last years. But Hillary described vividly his mother's last days. Gertrude was rushed to a hospital, where Ed went to spend time with her. In a matter of 15 minutes, he was beginning to fidget, as he had so often done in the past: Hillary loved action. Knowing her son as well as she did, Gertrude told him to go out and get some fresh air, which he did. Hours later she was dead. Hillary recalls in *View from the Summit*, "Why couldn't I have waited, even another miserable ten minutes, I kept asking myself? I have not always been thoughtful and kind, I fear."

Hillary began to contemplate his own life. As he approached 50, Hillary listed a handful of objectives. First, he wanted to improve his skiing. Second, he wished to complete a traverse climb of Mount Cook. Modest enough objectives for a man who was famous the world over. Instead, the losses kept coming.

Losing Louise and Belinda

Belinda, Hillary's youngest, had always been the apple of his eye. Although he was not outwardly affectionate, he loved his children. Belinda would jump into her father's arms, depositing all sorts of kisses. She was the only person who could break through his detachment.

In the autumn of 1975, Hillary was in the Solo Khumbu building another school. Rex had become an ace builder for Hillary's Himalayan Trust, and things were going very well, indeed. Louise and Belinda were flying in to meet him. When Hillary saw a helicopter approach, instead of a plane, he had a gnawing sense that something was wrong. He rushed to the helicopter pad and was greeted with the terrible news. Louise and Belinda, along with three other passengers, had all died in a crash soon after their plane took off from Katmandu.

Hillary went to Katmandu to identify the bodies. His daughter, Sarah, was quickly located, but it took some time to find Peter, who was then on a trekking expedition in India. When the surviving family members gathered, they stood by a roadside and wept. Life would never be the same, and they all knew it. Louise had been the anchor of the family, and Belinda had been the favorite.

As Sarah later expressed it to Hillary's authorized biographer, Alexa Johnston, in *Sir Edmund Hillary: An Extraordinary Life*:

> It was really a very terrible time. Some families get closer together and that helps, but I think in our family the two people who would probably have dealt with an accident much better had died. And the people who were left really couldn't cope very well, and we all spun off in our own individual directions.

Louise and Belinda were cremated in Nepal and their ashes were brought to New Zealand. Ed Hillary went into a serious depression that lasted for at least two years and, by some accounts, as many as five. He drank to excess, used sleeping pills frequently, and generally went about his tasks with a morbid feeling and a sullen will. He did not abandon any of his projects, but the joy and cheerfulness of the past were gone. It was around this time, in the depths of grief, that Hillary began to think of another adventure.

Mother Ganga

Sometime in the late 1960s, Hillary had become interested in rivers. It was a natural progression, as the great rivers of the world often have their beginnings in a small stream atop a

TENZING'S DIFFICULTIES

If Ed Hillary had to cope with being the hero of the Western world, then Tenzing Norgay had to handle being considered a demigod in some parts of the Eastern one. At the time of the 1953 climb, he vaulted to a status that can only be compared to that of a person landing on the moon: something that had not been accomplished until 1969.

Tenzing and his family wished to return to life as normal, but they found it quite impossible. He acted as a guide for many trekking expeditions in Nepal and cheerfully fielded questions about his 1953 feat, but the actions brought him less and less pleasure. By the 1970s, while Hillary had turned to alcohol to numb the pain of losing his wife and daughter, Tenzing had done the same in response to the pressures of worldwide fame.

Thankfully, both men had sons that revered their legacy and, in some ways, continued it.

mountain or glacier. In the year that followed his wife's and daughter's deaths, Hillary began thinking about the Ganges River (better known in India as Ganga or Mother Ganga).

For a mountaineer, it would make sense to imagine a journey from the river's source to its culmination in the great ocean. Hillary thought of the reverse, a journey from the estuary of the Ganges to its source, remote in the High Himalaya. Along the way, he and his fellows would experience the Ganges as it was meant to be, a source of spiritual enlightenment.

Finding friends and collaborators was not difficult. Hillary eventually had 15 people to accompany him. The method and the means were thornier problems. How does one ascend the river?

Pilgrims traditionally walked the Ganges, taking in the sights and sounds of a thousand villages along the way. This would take months, if not a full year. Hillary and his team decided on the use of boats, and jet ones at that.

The world's first jet boats were designed by the Hamilton Company of Christchurch, New Zealand. A powerful jet engine sucked in water at the very bottom of the boat, then discharged it at the rear, giving the engines the possibility of 45 miles (70 kilometers) per hour. More important, the jet boats had no propeller, nothing on which sand, seaweed, and refuse material would cling. A jet boat could carry its occupants quickly and relatively safely.

In the spring of 1977, although fund-raising efforts were underway for what they called the Ocean to Sky Expedition, Hillary laid out a good deal of money from his own earnings. If he did not purchase the boats now, it would be too late for travel during that season. The three boats—christened Ganga, Air India, and Kiwi—were Hamilton Jet 52s, 16 feet long, made of fiberglass, and equipped with V-8 engines. The yellow and green canopies, designed by Hillary, were supplied by Sears, Roebuck, and Co.

On August 24, 1977, the 16-man expedition gathered at the southeastern part of the Ganges Delta. They took the three jet boats down the coast for a visit to the Temple of Ganga Sagar, the traditional jumping-off point for all Ganges's pilgrimages. The small, wiry temple priest acted as if he saw jet boats every day. He blessed the boats and the men, giving official sanction to their pilgrimage.

The expedition returned to the delta and began zooming up the channels that blend and twist together to make the final aspect of Mother Ganga.

Upstream

The boats moved far more effectively than a traditional motorboat, which is equipped with a propeller, but there were still plenty of snags. Driftwood combined with seaweed and debris slowed down the boats and sometimes pulled them onto sandbars. Given the movement of water by jet, from under the boat to the rear, it was almost impossible to swamp the jet boats, but there were times when the whole expedition had to get into the water and give a mighty heave-ho to get the boat unstuck.

Even the magnificent canopies did not protect the passengers. As the jet boats picked up speed of more than 30 miles per hour, the passengers became thoroughly soaked. Yet everyone remained excited, and few of them complained. What surprised them most were the crowds.

In order to make this journey, Hillary had applied for, and received, permission from the Indian government. The media caught word of the expedition and, as the team moved upstream, it sometimes found as many as 50,000 people gathered in one spot, with hundreds, if not thousands, of hands begging for autographs. If Hillary had ever doubted his worldwide celebrity status, such thoughts were put to rest. Indian schoolchildren grew up reading about him and Tenzing atop Mount Everest.

Crowds sometimes meant danger. On one occasion, 30,000 people became hostile when an Indian policeman shoved a protestor with his rifle. Although no one was hurt, the scene had the potential to become a disaster. When someone asked Hillary to come through the barrier to shake the hand of the man who had been struck, Hillary recalled, "With a little trepidation I pushed my way over to the wall of the tent and grasped the man firmly by the hand. Immediately his anger evaporated; he broke into a broad smile, and shook my hand vigorously in return." The man and his friends turned friendly, but the crowd remained dangerous, so Hillary and his comrades beat a hasty retreat to the boats.

As the expedition progressed, Hillary noticed that the expedition members varied in their response to the crowds. Some liked the attention but became exhausted from it. Others found it too overwhelming. There was no way around it; surely, as they moved into rural India, the size of the crowds would lessen.

The size actually stayed large, but the rural crowds were more subdued. There were few incidents like the one experienced previously.

As the expedition moved upstream, the photographers took endless rolls and reels of film. This was before the invention of the Internet, and these documentary pictures would be vital to conveying the importance and value of the expedition.

There were amusing moments, such as when Hillary stood on the balcony at the home of a very famous maharaja (leader) who had entertained him back in 1953. The maharaja commented that Hillary had "decided to put on weight," to which Hillary replied that he was a little older. "A lot older, a lot older!" replied the maharaja.

Hillary was an old hand at experiences like this, which he usually took with excellent humor. Still, a growing sense of his mortality did accompany him on this journey. After all, his 20-year-old son, Peter, was there, brimming with the vitality of youth. Hillary had so many memories, so many triumphs to recall, but he could not force away the plain fact that he was well into middle age.

Midway

The expedition reached the midpoint at Varanasi, the city that is a prayer, as it is called. Although he had been raised a Presbyterian, Hillary had little belief in any formal religion. Still, he was as excited as any other expedition member by the temples of Varanasi and the passion and devotion of thousands of pilgrims. The waters of the Ganges are believed to wash away the sins of three lifetimes if one applies the right *puja*, or ceremony.

From Varanasi, the expedition progressed upstream to Hardwar. Hillary described this as the point where the Ganges changed from being a sluggish river meandering across farmers' fields to a "young mountain torrent, moving between rocky walls." Hillary and company noticed that the river was rising in altitude rather dramatically. Over the first thousand miles of their travel, the Ganges had risen by only about six inches per mile, but by the time they reached Hardwar, it was up to five or even ten feet per mile and still rising. This was part of the challenge, of course, and part of what had called Hillary to undertake this expedition in the first place. The jet boats, however, had more of a difficult time.

Finally, on September 29, the expedition had to leave the jet boats because they could no longer ascend or navigate the difficult stream. Hillary knew this region; he had been here on his very first Himalayan trip in 1951. He and five others, including Peter, set off to walk the remaining 60 miles.

The Source

Hillary and the others wanted to reach the tiny stream that issues from a glacier, known as the fount of the entire Ganges. But

In 1977, Hillary led Ocean to the Sky, an expedition to find the source of India's Ganges River (*above*). His team, which included his son, Peter, used jet boats to travel from the mouth of the river high up into the Himalayas. The team's successful climb to a peak they called Sky Peak was done without Hillary, who had to be evacuated due to high-altitude sickness.

as they ascended from 4,000 to 10,000 feet, expedition members noticed that Hillary was not his usual self. He wheezed a bit more than in the past and seemed more tired in the evenings. Peter more than compensated for Hillary's pace, though. He showed every ambition to become as skilled a mountaineer as his father.

As they approached Ganga Parbat (Ganges Mountain), Hillary's condition worsened. He had experienced altitude sickness before, on Makalu, but not this bad. One night, Hillary was beset by chills and a cough, and the next morning he could barely speak, let alone move. The expedition's doctor told them that altitude sickness either gets better rapidly or much worse. They had to do something fast. One member raced back to base camp to call for a helicopter. The other five decided not to wait. They lifted Hillary into a tent that they converted into a sleigh. At great risk of injury to themselves, they carried and pulled him down the mountainside. By evening they had descended 3,000 feet, and Hillary's skin began to resume the pink, healthy tone they all knew. The danger was largely past.

The helicopter arrived the next morning, and, against his will, Hillary was brought to a much lower location. He felt embarrassed, perhaps even humiliated, by his altitude sickness, but the Indian police and military were not going to let this world-famous man perish on their watch. They insisted he remain under their care.

With that, the Ocean to Sky Expedition of 1977 came to an end. Hillary and company had done great and wonderful things, and there was no shame to having been defeated by weather and altitude. Perhaps it was a sign of emerging maturity that Hillary accepted his defeat on Ganga Parbat. So close, and yet so far.

Rebirth

AS THE 1970S ENDED, HILLARY WAS NOT IN GREAT FORM. HE
had, to some extent, recovered from the crushing loss of his wife
and daughter, but he still was not the joyous man of previous
years. The Ocean to Sky Expedition had reminded him of his
old vigor, but it also showed he was no longer a man of 33—the
age at which he conquered Mount Everest. Now, in the fullness
of his years, he was about to embark on new adventures, one of
which would actually include wearing a suit and tie.

Peter and June Mulgrew

Hillary had many friends, collected from years spent in different locations. One of his closest and dearest friends was Peter
Mulgrew. They had shared the difficult attempt of Makalu in 1954,
and Peter had been part of the Old Firm that drove to the South
Pole in 1957–1958. Hillary and Peter had drifted apart over the
years, however. Around 1979, Hillary found himself becoming

closer with June, Peter's wife. She and Peter were separated; still, Hillary thought he and June were just good friends.

Then came a great tragedy.

Due to the exploits of Hillary and other Kiwi climbers, there was an increased interest in the Southern Alps of New Zealand. Flights over that region increased, with Hillary some-times acting as the narrator, right on the plane. This was to have been the case in November 1979, but Hillary had other

In 1989, at the age of 70, Hillary married June Mulgrew (*second from right*). She was also interested in Himalayan treks and with helping the Sherpa community. Both of them continued to raise funds and travel to the Everest region and many Sherpas thought of them as family. In 2003, Hillary was named an honorary citizen of Nepal.

commitments. Peter Mulgrew happily took Hillary's place. Hillary was in Chicago meeting with his American sponsors when he learned the terrible news. The plane had crashed on New Zealand's Mount Erebus, killing everyone onboard (275 people total).

Hillary flew back to New Zealand at once, feeling remorse over the way he and Peter had drifted apart. But he could not escape the fact that June was becoming more important to him. A vivacious beauty in youth, she had matured into a woman of great depth. She was also interested in Himalayan treks and in the building of schools for the Sherpas. Their friendship continued to grow.

Becoming High Commissioner

In 1984, Hillary was 64, and in all those years he had never held a nine-to-five job. Working the bees had been more athletic; trekking in the mountains had been heroic; and the building of schools required overalls and straw hats. Nonetheless, in the summer of 1984, he received his first job offer: high commissioner of New Zealand to India.

New Zealand and India were distant neighbors, and although there had been some tensions between the countries, there had been no high commissioner in residence in five years. In 1984, New Zealand voted in a new government, and the new prime minister, David Lange, offered the job to Hillary. Would he reestablish good relations with India?

Hillary was both pleased and shocked. A man with virtually no training in diplomacy and little interest in politics was being offered a top ambassador post. His only concern, which he expressed to the prime minister, was that he could not give up all of his nonprofit work in the Himalaya: He would need a month or two there each year. This was not a problem, and Ed Hillary, the beekeeper's son, became the ambassador to a foreign land.

Hillary also needed to consider his relationship with June Mulgrew. She eventually solved the matter for him, proposing that she might come along. The happy couple accepted the offer and went to India, where June's title was O.C., standing for "official companion."

Hillary and June arrived in New Delhi to find the former ambassador's residence in complete disarray, and it was here that June began to take control. A fine designer, she handled nearly all of the details, which allowed Hillary to concentrate on his work as New Zealand's official representative. This proved not to be difficult, because the average Indian had such a high opinion of Hillary. Here was the man who had climbed Mount Everest and traveled up the Ganges. New Zealand could not have been more fortunate in its choice. But even as he settled

A SELECT CLUB

Ed Hillary and Tenzing Norgay were perhaps the greatest world celebrities of the 1950s—known and recognized by all. Yet, they were only a part of a small, select club of twentieth-century explorers who received fame and attention, attention that far exceeded that given to their predecessors. Hillary would be the first to say that he had, perhaps, received too much attention.

Between 1900 and 1925, the greatest celebrity was accorded to those who tried to reach either the North or South Pole. Frederick E. Peary was the first to reach the North Pole in 1906, and Roald Amundsen was the first to reach the South Pole, in 1912. There were other monumental achievements that came after, however. Admiral Richard Byrd was the first man to fly over either the North or South Pole in 1926. And everyone knows the name Charles E. Lindbergh, the first person to fly solo over the Atlantic. When he landed at Paris's Bourget airport in 1927, Lindbergh became one of the most famous persons—including presidents, prime ministers, and dictators—of the time.

into the official residence, Hillary had yet another adventure to pull off before being named high commissioner. He had accepted an offer to fly to the North Pole with none other than the first person to land on the moon.

Hillary flew from India to Canada. By the time his trip was done, he had gone from 35 degrees above Celsius to 35 degrees below Celsius in just six days. He and his son, Peter, linked up with Neil Armstrong and three others in Canada, and together the six men flew to the North Pole by short hops. Upon landing, they brought out a bottle of champagne, which froze immediately! Hillary recalled the moment in *View from the Summit*:

> As I walked over the bumpy ice for a mile or so I thought
> how different it was from the South Pole which was at an

The Second World War got in the way of great exploration achievements, but men and women went to it with a passion after 1945. The first of the highest peaks was scaled in 1950; three years later, Hillary and Tenzing vaulted into the immortal position that remains. Just as polar exploration had yielded to airplanes and to mountain climbing, desire was ignited to see a person walk on the moon.

Neil Armstrong and Buzz Aldrin achieved this feat on July 20, 1969. Thanks to the miracle of telemetry (wireless communication) and the more mundane spectacle of television, their achievement was recorded for all time and was immediately relayed to millions of people around the globe. Armstrong was off the ladder first, and though he was a self-effacing person, his fame eclipsed that of Buzz Aldrin.

No one knew it in 1969, but the age of heroic exploration was about to be reborn in a new and exciting way: extreme sports. People around the globe now exhibit the desire to perform all sorts of enormous feats, such as rowing across the Atlantic, climbing Mount Everest without using oxygen, and the like. Far more people participate in these extreme sports than in the past.

What would Lindbergh, Hillary, and Armstrong think?

altitude of 9,300 feet. . . . I did have a considerable feeling of satisfaction—I believed I was the first person to have stood at both the North and South Poles and on the summit of Mount Everest.

The irony of transportation did not escape Hillary. He realized it was odd that he had reached Mount Everest on his own feet, the South Pole by Ferguson farm tractor, and the North Pole by small plane.

Hillary and Armstrong were congenial companions. Both were worldwide celebrities, and both were a bit embarrassed by the situation. On one evening, Hillary asked Armstrong how he had been selected for the mission to the moon, and the American astronaut replied, "Luck! Just luck!"

Both men knew there was more to it, but both also knew there was a kernel of truth within the modesty. Hillary and Tenzing had had the great fortune to be the first atop Mount Everest, but if weather conditions had been better, Charles Evans and Tom Bourdillon might have done it two days earlier. Armstrong and Buzz Aldrin were the first people on the moon, but there may have been a dozen other astronauts who could have done the job. Too often one forgets about astronaut Michael Collins, who circled the moon while his two fellows walked on it, and too often we forget that Hillary and Tenzing had to have the assistance of Sherpa porters, or else they would never have reached the summit.

Ed and Peter returned to India.

Tenzing Dies

Hillary was a major success as high commissioner to India. Much of this was due to his great status, but his modest demeanor and accommodating attitude also made the difference. June Mulgrew, as official companion, smoothed the way over many difficulties.

In 1986, Hillary was sad to learn that Tenzing had died. The two had grown closer in India, with Hillary learning that life had been rather difficult for Tenzing. As a Sherpa, born to the obscurity of the mountains, it was hard to accept the fame that arrived and even harder to meet the financial obligations that accompanied it. Tenzing had been lonely toward the end of his life, and he had bounced between alcoholism and periods of sobriety, a condition that Hillary could fully comprehend. Ed and June were the only people of European descent at Tenzing's funeral. His body was cremated and his spirit released to the sky.

Going Home

Hillary and June left India in the spring of 1989 and returned to New Zealand. Their children made the bold proposition that they should marry, which they did in November of that year. A striking couple they made—the tall, weather-beaten Ed Hillary and the radiant, white-haired June Mulgrew. Yet, if they thought they were all done with the world, or vice versa, they were sadly mistaken.

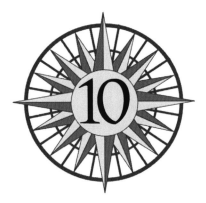

Fathers
and Sons

THE NEW ZEALAND CURRENCY NOW REFLECTED THE NATION'S greatest hero. The five-dollar note portrayed Hillary on one side and a yellow-eyed penguin on the other. When asked to comment about this, Hillary brushed the question aside, saying he didn't think a lot about it. Still, when called into action to help those in need, he continued to respond.

The Rescue of Thyangboche Monastery

Shortly before Hillary left India, Thyangboche Monastery, 15 miles southwest of Mount Everest, burned to the ground. The lamas and monks turned to the only person they felt certain could help.

Thyangboche (or Tengboche, as it is known today) was one of the most important places in Hillary's life. He remembered his first time there, in 1951, and his triumphant return there, in 1953. Since that time, there had been any number

Edmund Hillary was the first New Zealander to appear on that country's currency. He appears on the front of the five-dollar bill.

of visits to Thyangboche, and he was determined to make the place rise from the ashes.

As usual, his brother, Rex, was instrumental in the planning and reconstruction. Thyangboche did rise, slowly, and in the summer of 1993, Hillary was present at the rededication of the fabled monastery. Nothing could have made him happier, save perhaps an invitation from London.

Knight of the Garter

Though he was known around the world, especially so in English-speaking circles, Hillary had not received many invitations from Queen Elizabeth II. In 1993, he was asked to become a Knight of the Garter, the highest strata of British nobility. Hillary naturally accepted, and in June 1995 he was formally inducted into the circle that included his old comrade in arms, Sir John Hunt.

What did Hillary and Hunt discuss on that occasion? Did they marvel over the changes that had taken place in the world?

Did they discuss the changes in the sport of mountaineering? Either way, it would have been an intriguing dialogue.

Peter Hillary and Jamling Tenzing Norgay

In May 1990, at home in New Zealand, Hillary received a telephone call from his son, Peter, who quickly said that he was atop Mount Everest. By the miracle of modern communications, Peter's walkie-talkie signal was bounced down the mountain and then beamed by satellite all the way to Auckland.

Peter expressed his admiration for his father and Tenzing, who, as everyone knew, had reached the top with much less sophisticated equipment. He marveled at how his father and Tenzing had found their way over and through the Hillary Step. Peter eventually said his feet were chilly and that he must hang up.

Ed Hillary was not much given to introspection, but the phone call may have prompted his recognition of life coming full circle. In 1953, when he and Tenzing reached the top, it had taken two days to get to Base Camp and two more days for the world to know. Now, in 1990, Peter was able to reach him instantaneously.

Meanwhile, Tenzing Norgay's son, Jamling Tenzing Norgay, was striking out on his own. Jamling had been deeply affected by his father's death in 1986, and he hoped that the tenth anniversary of that occasion would be a triumphant return to the mountain. It happened that no less than four expeditions were scheduled for Mount Everest that May—Taiwanese, Japanese, South African, and American—and the approaches to the mountain were, to say the least, crowded. On May 10, 1996, Jamling and the climbers he was with witnessed a horrific scene: Eight climbers died, thousands of feet above them, and there was no way to offer any help. One man, miraculously, staggered off the mountain.

Jamling had received negative predictions from a lama he deeply trusted, and, after the terrible tragedy, he debated whether to proceed. A phone call to his wife, in Katmandu, persuaded him to go on, and on May 20, 1996, he and four other members of the American expedition stood atop Mount Everest. In his autobiography, *Touching My Father's Soul*, Jamling confessed that he had been torn between traditional Sherpa beliefs and the Western ones he had encountered while in college in the United States. Yet coming to grips with the great mountain—and experiencing the tragedy that happened that year—reaffirmed many of his Sherpa teachings and made the struggle and sacrifice of his father more real for him.

Peter Hillary, meanwhile, was out to set some records of his own.

Photographs from the 1980s and 1990s show a man who strongly resembled his father, both in lanky fitness and in outdoor vigor. Peter and his father had gone through periods when they were less than close. (Ed Hillary later wrote that the May 1990 telephone call from Everest was the longest conversation he had had with Peter in some time.) Still, as the twenty-first century began, a new bond developed between father and son, shown both by commemorations of Ed's accomplishments and a growing sense of wonder in Peter's.

In May 2002, Peter and Tenzing Norgay's grandson, Tashi, climbed Everest, and in 2003, members of both families were on hand to celebrate the golden (fiftieth) anniversary of the great event of 1953. Ed Hillary was justified in saying that Peter was "a very effective chip off the old block." In 2008, Peter achieved his goal of climbing the Seven Summits—the highest peaks on each of the world's continents.

1. Everest: 29,028 feet (8,848 meters), Nepal/Tibet (1990, 2002)

2. Aconcagua: 22,837 feet (6,961 meters), Argentina, South America (1991)
3. Vinson Massif: 16,066 feet (4,897 meters), Ellsworth Range, Antarctica (1992)
4. Carstenz Pyramid: 16,020 feet (4,883 meters), Indonesia, Oceania (1995)
5. Kilimanjaro: 19,340 feet (5,895 meters), Tanzania, Africa (2005)
6. Elbrus: 18,480 feet (5,633 meters), Russia, Europe (2006)
7. McKinley: 20,321 feet (6,194 meters), Alaska, North America (2008)

Hillary's Last Years

Ed Hillary's last years were a mixture of joy and sorrow. He saw the decline and departure of many old friends and family members, including his brother, Rex, who died in 2004. Rex had never tried to be in the public eye, but he had been an enormous source of help to his brother, going back to the days when they tended bees together. It was Rex who kept the apiaries going while Ed climbed the mountains, and it was Rex who did much of the practical planning of building schools for the Himalayan Trust.

Ed and June seemed like mountains of strength in their final years, betraying few physical weaknesses, but Ed's lecture tour slowed down, and they spent more time at home than in the past. When interviewed, Ed usually had high praise for young people and their efforts, but he did occasionally express disdain for what had changed in the art of mountaineering. When a New Zealand expedition left a member behind in 2004 and a climber perished, Hillary expressed scorn for the new mountaineering ethic that placed getting to the top over the well-being of a team member.

Ed Hillary died in Auckland on January 11, 2008.

FRUITS OF A LIFETIME

Ed Hillary was always proud of his individual accomplishments. He knew what it meant to be one of the great explorers of his time. He was, perhaps, even prouder of what he had done over the course of 40 years for the Sherpa people.

It all began with that conversation in which a village elder told him that "our children have eyes, but they are still blind." The first "Hillary school" was completed in 1961, and 25 others followed over the decades, with Ed Hillary doing most of the planning and a fair bit of the actual work. Many Sherpas continue to live traditional lives after graduation, but some have gone far afield; one pilots jumbo jets today, while another works for wildlife conservation in Washington, D.C. And there are the hospitals.

When Hillary first came to the Himalaya, about 50 percent of all Sherpas died before the age of 20. That has changed, both through a vaccination program and through making iodine available to the Sherpa people. Hillary was instrumental in planning six hospitals and a scattering of small clinics throughout the Solo Khumbu. The results have been astonishing. The Sherpas now enjoy medical care roughly equivalent to that of city-dwellers in far-off places.

Of course this has come at a cost. One of Hillary's few regrets was building an airstrip in the Solo Khumbu, which led to a massive influx of trekkers and mountain climbers. The visitors use more firewood in a week than a traditional Sherpa family did in a year, leading to deforestation. Hillary did his best to change this with the creation of Sagamartha National Park in 1986.

Anyone who does good deeds becomes aware of their unintended consequences. Hillary's work has been justly hailed as some of the most important of his time, for one can search the record without finding a parallel to this explorer, driven by his own desire, who then converted that desire into a lasting love for the people whose labors made it possible.

To mark the occasion of the fiftieth anniversary of the first successful ascent of Mount Everest, celebrations were held in Nepal on May 29, 2003. The first man and the first woman to conquer the mountain, Sir Edmund Hillary and Japan's Junko Tabei, were in attendance along with renowned mountaineers from around the world.

Hillary Among the Explorers

Ed Hillary stands in the very top rank of explorers, of his time or any other. Certainly, one can point out that he had better equipment in the 1950s than Irving and Mallory had in 1924, but it was not that much better. By contrast, the difference between the boots, shoes, and parkas of 1950 and those of today resembles a light-years comparison. It is true that he did not fulfill all his goals; in 1977, for example, he did not reach the very source of the Ganges River. But in terms of physical grit and resourceful planning, he must be reckoned among the truly great explorers of human history. Few great mountaineers have been fine organizers: Hillary was both. Even fewer mountaineers have become symbols of humanity's desire to excel (Mallory was Hillary's equal in this regard). Very few sportsmen have been as able to shift roles. Hillary went from beekeeper to soldier to explorer to pilgrim to philanthropist, and he did it all with class and style. If one anecdote can be used to epitomize his personal style, let it be this one:

In 1959, Hillary went to Chicago to meet with leaders of Field Enterprises. They later sponsored an expedition to find the Abominable Snowman. They

> expected the world-famous mountaineering knight to sweep in flanked by lawyers and accountants, but Ed arrived on his own: 'hair all over the place, and carrying an old briefcase tied together with string. Well that threw us right from the start. And when we came to the bit where we asked him how much he would like for himself and he says, 'Well, on an expedition we don't usually take any money for ourselves.'

The old briefcase was replaced by a new one, a gift from Field Enterprises. The expedition was funded. But most of all, Hillary showed himself as he was, a down-to-earth bloke (the New Zealand equivalent for "chap") who never took himself too seriously. Hopefully, there will be future Edmund Hillarys, men who do daring and remarkable things. The world will be fortunate if they, like him, see themselves as ordinary people doing extraordinary things.

CHRONOLOGY

1919	Edmund Percival Hillary born in Auckland.
1935	Hillary has his first taste of snow and skiing.
1939	World War II begins.
1945	Hillary injured in motorboat accident.
1947	Hillary and Ayres climb Mount Cook.
1951	Hillary and three other New Zealanders go to the Garhwal Himalaya.

TIMELINE

1919

Edmund Hillary born on July 2 in Auckland, New Zealand

Hillary and Ayres climb Mount Cook

1947

1953

Hillary and Tenzing reach summit of Mount Everest; Hillary marries Louise Rose on September 3

Hillary and his team reach the South Pole

1958

Hillary and friends dedicate a school in Nepal, the first of many he helped to build

1961

1951   Teams with Eric Shipton in British reconnaissance expedition to Everest.

1952   Hillary and mates fail to scale Cho Oyu.

1953   Hillary and Tenzing Norgay reach summit of Everest on May 29.

Hillary and John Hunt knighted by Queen Elizabeth. Marries Louise Rose.

1957-1958   Becomes first overland explorer to reach South Pole since Robert F. Scott.

1961   Builds first school in Solo Khumbu.

1975   Wife and daughter Belinda are killed in plane crash.

1977   Leads jet-boat expedition, called Ocean to Sky, to find the source of the Ganges River in India.

Louise and Belinda Hillary die in plane crash in Nepal on March 31

Hillary and Neil Armstrong reach North Pole on April 6

Hillary dies in Auckland on January 11

1977

1989

1975

1985

2008

Hillary and his team begin their journey up the Ganges

Marries June Mulgrew

1979	Friend Peter Mulgrew killed in plane crash on Mount Erebus.
1983	Thirtieth anniversary of ascent of Everest.
1984	Named high commissioner to India.
1985	Reaches North Pole with Neil Armstrong and son, Peter.
1989	Marries June Mulgrew.
1990	Peter Hillary ascends Everest.
1996	Son of Tenzing Norgay, Jamling Tenzing Norgay, ascends Everest.
1997	Grandson of Tenzing Norgay, Tashi Tenzing, ascends Everest.
2002	Peter Hillary and Tashi Tenzing ascend Everest each for second time.
2003	Fiftieth anniversary of ascent of Everest.
2008	Edmund Hillary dies in Auckland.
	Peter Hillary climbs Mount McKinley, completing the last of his Seven Summit series (climbing the highest peak on each of the seven continents).

GLOSSARY

BELAY, A   the projection itself: a rock, an axe, or even ice

BELAY, TO   to secure the climber's ropes to a firm projection that will secure him while moving through dangerous areas

COL   depression in a mountain range (used by George Mallory to describe the area between the Lhotse Face and Mount Everest)

CRAMPONS   metal frames with spikes, fitting the soles of the boot

CREVASSE   a fissure in a glacier, often of great depth

CWM   an enclosed valley on the flank of a hill

PUJA   ceremony of blessing, to ask for spiritual assistance

SHERPA   A Nepalese people who have acted as porters for many mountain-climbing expeditions

SIRDAR   leader of the Sherpas on an expedition

SOLO KHUMBU   the section of Nepal in which the Sherpas live

BIBLIOGRAPHY

Coburn, Broughton. *Triumph on Everest: A Photobiography of Sir Edmund Hillary*. Washington, D.C.: National Geographic, 2003.

Field, Michael. "The Dark Shadow over Sir Edmund's Life," The *Dominion Post*, January 11, 2008.

Fothergill, Alistair. *Planet Earth as You've Never Seen It Before*. Berkeley: University of California Press, 2007.

Gillman, Peter and Leni Gillman. *The Wildest Dream: The Biography of George Mallory*. Seattle: Mountaineers Books, 2000.

Hillary, Edmund. *High Adventure: The True Story of the First Ascent of Everest*. New York: E.P. Dutton & Company, 1955.

——— . *View from the Summit: The Remarkable Memoir by the First Person to Conquer Everest*. New York: Pocket Books, 1999.

Johnston, Alexa. *Sir Edmund Hillary: An Extraordinary Life*. New York: Penguin Books, 2005.

Keiser, Anne B. and Cynthia Russ Ramsay. *Sir Edmund Hillary and the People of Everest*. Kansas City: Andrews McMeel Publishing, 2002.

King, Michael. *After the War: New Zealand Since 1945*. London: Hodder & Stoughton, 1988.

Mortenson, Greg and David Oliver Relin. *Three Cups of Tea: One Man's Mission to Promote Peace...One School at a Time*. New York: Penguin Books, 2006.

Norgay, Jamling Tenzing with Broughton Coburn. *Touching My Father's Soul: A Sherpa's Journey to the Top of Everest*. San Francisco: HarperCollins, 2001.

Norgay, Tenzing with James Ramsey Ullman. *Tiger of the Snows*. New York: G.P. Putnam's Sons, 1955.

Shipton, Eric. *The Mount Everest Reconnaissance Expedition*. New York: E.P. Dutton & Company, 1952.

FURTHER RESOURCES

Hemmleb, Jochen, et. al. *Ghosts of Everest: The Search for Mallory and Irvine*. Seattle: Mountaineers Books, 2001.

Hillary, Edmund. *Nothing Venture, Nothing Win*. New York: Pocket Books, 1999.

Jenkins, Steve. *The Top of the World: Climbing Mount Everest*. New York: Houghton Mifflin, 1999.

Krakauer, Jon. *Into Thin Air: A Personal Account of the Mount Everest Disaster*. New York: Anchor Books, 1999.

The Royal Geographic Society. *Everest: Summit of Achievement*. New York: Simon and Schuster, 2003.

WEB SITES

Everest News

http://www.everestnews.com/

Everest news coverage for mountain climbers.

The Himalayan Trust

http://www.himalayantrust.co.uk/index.phtml

Charity developed by Sir Edmund Hillary to support projects for the hills people of Nepal.

Mount Everest History and Facts

http://www.mnteverest.net/history.html

Facts and history about the tallest mountain in the world.

National Geographic—Everest

http://www.nationalgeographic.com/everest/

Information, images, links to other sites, and articles about Mount Everest.

Peakbagger.com
http://peakbagger.com/climber/ClimbListC.aspx?cid=144
Ascent List for Edmund Hillary.

Tengboche Monastery Development Project
http://www.tengboche.org/introduction.htm
The official site for the Tengboche Monastery Development Project with information about Buddhism, ecology, and sustainable tourism in the Sherpa region of Mount Everest.

PICTURE CREDITS

INDEX

About
the Author

SAMUEL WILLARD CROMPTON lives in the Berkshire Hills of Massachusetts (average of between 1,000 and 2,500 feet), but he has never climbed a real mountain. He is the author or editor of many books, including two others in the GREAT EXPLORERS series. Crompton teaches history at Westfield State College and Holyoke Community College, where he observes a keen interest on the part of young people for mountain climbing, sky-diving, and the like.